MONEY IS EASY

How to increase
prosperity, attract riches,
experience abundance,
and have more money!

Larry Winget

Praise for
Money Is Easy

"With Money Is Easy *everyone now has the principles for creating abundance in all areas of life. No one has to settle for poverty ever again. Larry's book is a powerful contribution to the world!"*

Michael Wickett, author
It's All Within Your Reach

"You'll love reading Money Is Easy. *Larry Winget is a genius of an author. He makes learning the principles of attracting massive amounts of money irresistibly interesting, understandable, fun, and instantly do-able. The great news is that you'll go from shortage to surplus and lack to lots. You'll be thanking Larry Winget in your prayers for giving you time and money and freedom, thanks to this book."*

Mark Victor Hansen, author
How To Achieve Total Prosperity,
co-author *Chicken Soup For The Soul*

Printed in the United States of America.

Cover and inside design by Ad Graphics, Tulsa, Oklahoma.

Library of Congress Catalog Number: 93-094054

ISBN: 1-881342-21-2

"Money Is Easy™" is a trademark of Win Publications!, Win
Seminars!, and Larry Winget, denoting a series of books and
products including pocket cards, calendars, audio cassettes and
videotapes.

Published by:
Win Publications!
a subsidiary of Win Seminars!, Inc.
P. O. Box 700485
Tulsa, Oklahoma 74170
918 745-6606

Order information:
Win Publications!
P. O. Box 700485
Tulsa, Oklahoma 74170
Call Toll Free:

800 749-4597

Publisher's Cataloging in Publication Data

Winget, Larry
    Money Is Easy: how to increase prosperity, attract riches,
experience abundance and have more money! / Larry Winget.
    p. cm.
    Includes bibliographical references.
    Preassigned LCCN: 93-094054.
    ISBN 1-881342-21-2

    J. Finance, Personal. I.Title.
HG179.W454 1994   332.024
                                   QB194-582

Also by
Larry Winget

The Simple Way To Success

Just Do This Stuff

Stuff That Works Every Single Day

The Little Red Book Of Stuff That Works!

Profound Stuff

Success One Day At A Time

Only The Best On Success

Only The Best On Customer Service

Only The Best On Leadership

That Makes Me Sick!

Contents

Special thanks to:

Brian Tracy, Mike Wickett, Mark Victor Hansen, Ernest Holmes, Jack Boland, Mariannne Williamson, Dr. Wayne Dyer, Dr. Deepak Chopra, Catherine Ponder, Emmet Fox, Arnold Patent, Eric Butterworth, Frederick J. Eikerenkoetter II, Bob Proctor, Florence Scovel Shinn, Jerry Gillies, Jim Rohn, Dr. Robert Schuller, The Unity Church, The Church of Religious Science and Science of Mind.

A party gives laughter,
and wine gives happiness;
but money gives everything.

Ecclesiastes 10:19
Living Bible

Introduction To Money Is Easy

Let's get one thing straight from the start. I know that money is only one part of success. I know that balance is critically important in life. I know that if your goal in life is just to make money, you will ultimately lose everything that is really important. I know that there are lots of people who are very happy and never accumulate very much money. I know that there are people who have millions of dollars and are totally miserable. I know all of that stuff. In fact, I wrote my first book, <u>The Simple Way To Success</u>, explaining all of this and more.

And! I also know that it sure helps to have some money! I know that I can help the world a lot more when I have money. I know that I can serve my church, my community, my family, and my world better when I give them my very best in terms of service and love and throw in some money too. And while money is not success, success certainly does include at least some money!

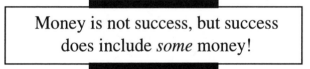

Money is not success, but success
does include *some* money!

Now that we've gotten that out of the way, let's get to the point of this book: helping you get more money. This book is full of principles for attracting money into your life. Principles that work. I know they do. I've used them and they've worked for me. That is not to say that I have mastered them. I haven't. In fact, I'm learning more every day. And it doesn't mean that I have lots and lots of money. I don't. Some might say that it would have been better to wait until I had millions in the bank before writing a book about how to get rich. I would have probably had more credibility and an even larger readership. But could you have waited? No! You want more money right now. You deserve more money right now. And you deserve to start learning about how to get it right now.

All that any of this means is that I've found out **some** of what it takes to become the right kind of person, believing the right stuff, and doing the right stuff that will allow me to get the money that I want, need and deserve. When I learn more stuff, I'll write another book. But until then, I couldn't wait to share this stuff and you can't wait any longer to get it.

How do I know this stuff about money? I've had it and I've not had it and I've decided that it's better to have it. I spent a good portion of my life not having much of it. I came from a family with a very modest income. I grew up hearing about all the stuff we couldn't afford. I thought that having lots of money was for the other people. While my parents had great attitudes about life, and they did know how to enjoy the money they had, I know now their attitudes about money kept them from having a whole lot of it.

When I got out of college, I got a good job with AT&T, got several promotions and made a pretty good living; not a great living, but a pretty good living. After ten years with AT&T, and having received many promotions, I found myself in a position that I no longer enjoyed and in a city that I didn't care for. So I took an early retirement package that the company was offering and left AT&T to move back to my Home-Sweet-Oklahoma. At that point, I started my own telecommunications company. I really had no business going into business. I had no seed capital and no knowledge of what it took to really run a business, but I was a great salesman. So through hard work, determination, a dream, and the help of some good people, I grew that company into a real success. I started making really good money and finally knew what it was like to be a financial success.

Then through a series of bad hiring decisions, a turn in the economy, a growing lack of interest in the telecommunications industry, my dissatisfaction with the company, my personal desire to do something else with my life, and a bunch of really stupid mistakes, my company went from being a real success to a total disaster. The company went into bankruptcy. As the company's founder and president, and the guy with his name on all of the dotted lines, I went into bankruptcy right along with it.

Sad story, right? Wrong. I earned that bankruptcy. I created it. I deserved it. And it became the best thing that ever happened to me. I learned more in that one experience than I did in all of my years of education, and in all my years of working for someone else. I learned valuable lessons that became the foundation of my speaking career. I learned the principles of success. I learned that it's not what happens to you that really matters, it's what you do about what happens to you that really matters. I learned about loving what you do and doing what you love. And I learned that being broke is the pits!

That's when I started really examining what it takes to attract money. I started to build my personal and professional life on principles. I started to earnestly study success and prosperity. I had to. Even after the bankruptcy, I had hundreds of thousands of dollars worth of debt to pay off and no job.

At that point I decided — no, actually Life had decided that I was going to be a full-time professional speaker. That is a career that doesn't have a regular paycheck, especially at first. While I struggled in the beginning, I learned the most important lessons of my life. Lessons that would become the message that I now have the privilege of sharing all around the world. Lessons that I am going to share with you in this book.

That entire story brings me to this point. This is where I need to be right now. This is exactly where you need to be right now. Otherwise, **neither** of us would be here.

Warning!

This book is more than a book about money. It is a book about my personal journey. A journey from lack to abundance. Not only material abundance, but abundance in the areas of happiness, satisfaction, peace of mind, health, relationships, understanding, and wholeness. Abundance is more than money. It is a life that is wonderfully full and overflowing with all of the good stuff.

The principles I am sharing in this book reflect my journey. They are a reflection of the transition I made from a WIIFM (What's-In-It-For-Me) Thinking to a WIIFT (What's-In-It-For-Them) Thinking. It is reflective of how my thoughts and desires moved from a motive of *get* to a motive of *give*.

This transition could be called many things by some people who are on the outside of True Understanding. But for me, this transition can only be called, Spiritual.

This new way of thinking and believing was not easy for me. I had to throw away years of dogma in order to reach this new freedom. However, it all made sense when I read one line by Ernest Holmes:

Ignorance stays with us until the day of enlightenment, until our vision toward the Spirit broadens and casts out the image of a no longer useful littleness.

I had thinking in my life that I was desperately holding on to because I had been conditioned into thinking it to be true. Even when I started to question it and doubt it, I held on. Then I read that one line and realized that I had a lot of "no longer useful littleness." That's when I started to let go of those things that simply weren't serving me. Things that were not moving me closer to where I wanted to be, but were either moving me away from where I wanted to be or causing me to be stuck in the same place. That's when I released myself to a much more fulfilling life.

A sigh of relief!

While this is a story of my personal journey, I am not going to tell you my life story. While this journey has been spiritual in nature for me, I am not going to be religious or preachy or even too spiritual.

A promise.

My promise is to give you sound practical principles that will help you attract riches, experience prosperity, and have more money! The principles in this book, when believed and acted upon will make you more money!

> The principles in this book,
> when believed and acted upon
> will make you more money!

The book.

This is not a long, complicated book. The chapters are short. It is a quick read. It is meant to be that way. The reason is that the principles for attaining money are really quite simple. I have done my best to state them in a straightforward manner and to have these ideas be as realistic and usable as I possibly can make them.

I have also used lots of quotes in this book. The reason is even more simple: I like them. To me, a quote is a mini-seminar. It is a complete lesson delivered in one or two sentences. Besides, there is just no way to improve on the way some things are said, so I didn't even try.

This is not a book that could be titled, "How To Get Rich In Ten Easy Lessons." This is a book dealing with the development of a life style that reflects a belief system based on the principles of prosperity that are universal, tried, tested, and true. So how quickly will it work? You get to decide that. The quicker you implement this life style the quicker the pay-off will be. Your prosperity is totally in your own hands.

How life works.

Whatever we create in consciousness, we will experience in our life.

Dr. Robert Anthony

For as he thinks in his heart, so is he.

Proverbs 23:7

Sooner or later you act out what you really think.

Japanese Proverb

All that a man achieves and all that he fails to achieve is the direct result of his own thoughts.

James Allen

Your outer world of form and experience is a reflection of your inner world of thoughts and feelings. As above, so below. As within, so without. That is a Law.

John Randolph Price

This is the biggy: figuring out how life really works. I was confused for so long. First, I wandered aimlessly just taking life as it came and living "with the breaks." Then, I became a "goal fiend." I would set goals and write goals and think goals. Yet, I still wasn't "getting it." I somehow knew there was more to it than that. That's when through my reading and thinking and experiences that it all started to come together. That's when I finally figured out the way life really works.

Results are everything!

That's right. Results are everything. I had a co-worker years ago who would say, "they don't ask how, they ask how many." How true. People don't really care what you do, they care what you get done. In any business venture, it only matters what the results are. Results are bankable. It's the same way in life. It doesn't matter what you say you are going to do or what you plan to do, it matters what you get done.

Most people, once they understand that results are everything, begin to focus totally on results. Salespeople think quota all the time. Goal fiends, like I was, think house, new car, certain dollar amounts, custom-made suits, or any number of other goals that can be set. We have all been taught to think results, results, results, without understanding that there is a process for achieving those results.

So what is really important is not so much the understanding of the importance of results, but the understanding of how we actually get results.

How we get results.

Results come about as a *result* of your actions. Your actions determine what kind of results you get. Good or bad. Like it or not, you always get results. It's really very simple. If you want to have more, you only have to do more. And everyone can do more. No matter how much you are currently doing, you can always do more. Even if it's just a little bit more. And here is the good news: if you just understand this much you can improve your results! This idea alone will improve your results and make you more money. It won't make you rich, but it will make you more.

Like it or not, you always get results!

The magic key.

Magic happens when you understand the next part of the process: when you realize what determines your actions. Your actions are determined by your beliefs.

> Results are determined by actions.
> Actions are determined by beliefs.

Memorize this. It will change your life!

This idea works in all areas of your life.

If you think you were born a winner, then you will act with the confidence of a winner and bring about winning results.

If you believe that the world is a terrible place and that people are basically bad and out to get you, then you will be untrusting and paranoid and people will take advantage of you and your world will be a terrible place.

If you think of yourself as a fat person, regardless of how much or how little you weigh, then you will take on the actions of a fat person and end up fat.

If you believe that the only way to be successful is to work hard all of your life and "pay your dues," then you will indeed work hard and pay a lot of dues in order to become successful.

And if you believe that life is *for* you and that you can be prosperous, then you will act that way and end up with that as your result.

This is how it works in business too. If a company wants to improve its results, the leaders will make up signs stating company goals and post them for everyone to see, thus getting the employees to focus on the goals. The more enlightened companies and leaders will go to the next level of understanding and design a plan of action to assure that the right things are being done to achieve those goals.

They know that when you change actions then you change results. (By the way, one definition of insanity is to expect different results from the same behavior.)

However, in the truly enlightened company, leaders understand that in order to change results they will have to go the next level and focus on the belief system of their employees. They know that if they can change the belief system of their people, then their actions will be a natural outpouring of their beliefs and the desired results will automatically occur.

It sounds simple doesn't it? It is. However, it is the hardest thing I ever tried to put into actual practice. Years of conditioning had to be broken in order to make this simple process a principle of practice in my life. I am reminded of the quote, "The chains of habit are too weak to feel, until they are too strong to break." That is the case with this principle. We have had it engrained within us to focus on results and actions and then our beliefs and thinking will follow along. That is backwards thinking and will only bring backwards results.

This principle has taught me that when my results aren't what I want them to be and what I know they should be and could be, that I must go back to the real flow of the process and ask myself what my belief system is about the issue. When my beliefs are right, my actions will be right and I will get the right results.

Beliefs — Actions — Results

A tough lesson to learn.

Your results, the ones you are experiencing right now, have been determined solely by your current belief system. At this point, you may be saying, "You mean I really believe that I deserve to be broke?" Yes. "I really believe that this old clunker is the right car for me?" Yes. "I really believe that I'm supposed to be miserable and hate my job?" Yes. "How can you say that?!!!?!!!!?" Simple. If you didn't believe it, then it wouldn't be that way for you. If those weren't your beliefs, then you wouldn't have those results.

There are no exceptions to this, so stop trying to find them. Don't waste your energy or your emotions trying to dispute this fact. This is a Law.

> Your results have been determined by your beliefs. Change your beliefs and you will change your results.

A paradox.

Give up your ties to results. One more time. Give up your ties to results. "But you said that results are everything." That's right, I did. And they are. Now give up all ties to them. Know what results you want. Put together a plan of action as best you can to achieve those results. Then give up your ties to results and focus on your belief system. Identify your belief system. Examine it. Question it. Change it if necessary. Then stay focused on the belief system and not the plan and not the results.

> Give up all ties to results!

Money is an effect. When you concentrate on the effect, you are forgetting the cause, and when you forget the cause, the effect begins to diminish. When you focus your attention on getting money, you are actually shutting off your supply.

John Randolph Price

The goal should not be to make money or acquire things, but to achieve the consciousness through which the substance will flow forth when and as you need it.

Eric Butterworth

The problem with goal setting.

I said earlier that I used to be a "goal fiend." I really was. In fact, I wrote a chapter in my book, <u>The Simple Way To Success</u>, all about goal setting and its importance. I also wrote another book called <u>Success One Day At A Time</u> that is all about goal setting and achievement. I still believe very much in goal setting and think that you should do it. However, I believe there is a problem with most goal setting programs. Most teach you to focus on the goal, with some asking you to focus on the plan. Wrong focus. I believe that you must focus on your beliefs.

If you set a goal to earn a million dollars and put together a sound plan that when implemented will get you a million dollars, yet don't really believe that you can do it or that you deserve a million dollars, then I'm convinced that you won't get the million dollars. Or if you get it, you won't be able to hold on to it. It is best to become a millionaire in your belief system first, then go after the million dollars.

Let's say you set a goal to weigh 175 pounds and you currently weigh 210 pounds. If you focus every day on the 175 pounds and eat all of the right stuff, yet deep inside really think of yourself as a fat person, then you will probably never weigh 175 pounds. At least not for long.

See how it works? Goals are great. You should have goals. In fact, you should have lots of goals. I have hundreds of them. I know what direction I want my life to take. I have identified certain things that I want to be, do and have. You should do the same. However, I encourage you to understand how you are going to reach any goal that you set: by having the right belief system.

Another problem with focusing on results.

When you focus on results you are limiting yourself to the results that *you* have in mind.

I have found that my own limiting self-concept and belief system just won't reward me in the same way that a Loving Universe will. I have learned that the Universe will reward me in bigger and better ways than I could ever reward myself.

I used to post signs in my office with dollar amounts and numbers of speeches to book so my Marketing Director and I would have something to shoot for. Later, I discovered that those signs, which reflected my limited focus, were actually getting in the way of my making much more money and booking many more speeches with much less effort.

Don't limit your good by imposing the limiting goal of a desired outcome. In the words of Jack Boland, "Don't let your good become the enemy of your better."

Set a goal, make it specific, and write it down, but use it only as a guideline. Never think of it as the ultimate achievement. Focus on the belief system and leave the reward up to the Universe.

The problem with The Plan.

Another problem with goal setting is The Plan. There are times that you simply won't have one. Times when you have no idea how you would go about achieving a certain thing. That's okay. Know what you want and focus on the belief that you can get it because you deserve it. Know that having it or being it or doing it will serve yourself and others well, and then the plan will work itself out.

Plans are also limiting. That's because no plan was ever designed that was implemented exactly the way it was laid out. It always requires a certain amount of change. And change is the thing that we are least comfortable with. So don't frustrate yourself with a plan that is so detailed it will drive you crazy trying to implement it. Plus, designing such a plan will only slow you down and hold up your reaching the goal. Remember these words of General George S. Patton, "A good plan violently executed right now is far better than a perfect plan executed next week."

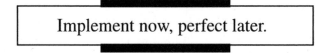

> **Implement now, perfect later.**

Use goal setting to identify where you want to be, what you want to do, and what you want to have. Use goals as guidelines. Have some idea of how you would go about accomplishing them. Then put your real effort into focusing on your belief system. That's when you will see amazing results.

So . . .

In terms of money, let me put it this way so there are no misunderstandings: in order to get more money - give up your ties to money! Instead:

> **Focus on a belief system of serving and loving others through your life, your love, your words, your product and service, and great quantities of money will come!**

CHAPTER

2

Believe.

If you can believe, all things are possible to him who believes.
Mark 9:23

The size of your success is determined by the size of your belief.
Dr. David J. Schwartz

The science of getting rich is based on the law of belief.
Joseph Murphy

According to your faith let it be to you.
Matthew 9:29

Prosperity consciousness is a positive belief system.
Jerry Gillies

They conquer who believe they can.
Ralph Waldo Emerson

No one is ready for a thing until he believes he can acquire it. The state of mind must be belief, not mere hope or wish.
Napoleon Hill

In the previous chapter, I explained how life works and the process for getting the results that you want. I discussed the importance that belief makes in your results. So now you are probably wondering what you should believe. Here are my suggestions:

Believe in yourself.

It's not what you are that holds you back, it's what you think you're not.
Dr. Denis Waitley

Henceforth I ask not good fortune. I myself am good fortune.
Walt Whitman

I am the greatest!

Muhammed Ali

You cannot perform in a manner that is inconsistent with your own self image.

William James

The true nature of our universe is that it is a field of all possibilities. In our most primordial state we are a field of all possibilities.

Dr. Deepak Chopra

People will pay you money to a great extent based on what value you place on yourself.

Jack Boland

In the middle of my financial disaster, I decided that I needed a few days away from it all. So I took my two boys to Dallas, Texas to Six Flags Over Texas, an amusement park. We played all day on Saturday and stayed over Saturday night so I could take my boys to hear Zig Ziglar teach his Sunday School Class at the First Baptist Church of Dallas. I really wanted my boys, Patrick and Tyler, who were six and ten at the time to have the experience of Zig in person. Zig had made a real difference in my thinking and started me on a road to being a more positive person.

When we got to the church I dragged them down front to meet Zig. Zig dropped to one knee in front of the boys and turned to look at me and said, "Larry, you've got yourself two winners here, I can spot 'em every time and I'm never wrong." Then he turned back to the boys and said, "You can be whatever you want to be, do whatever you want to do, go wherever you want to go, and have whatever you want to have, as long as you believe in yourself." My boys smiled and we went back to our seats.

About three months later, the three of us were out taking my two dogs, Elvis and Nixon, for a walk when my six year old, Patrick, turned to me and said, "Dad, what are you going to do?" He had noticed that I hadn't been doing very much. I didn't have a company any more. I didn't have a job. He had also noticed that things had changed considerably around our house. He had been there when my big fancy car was repossessed. He was with me when I sold my Rolex watch with the diamond bezel at the pawn shop. He was there when we had a garage sale every weekend in order to pay the bills. So his question, "Dad, what are you going to do?" made good sense to him at the time.

I said, "Patrick, I don't know what I'm going to do." He said, "Dad, why don't you just remember what Zig told me?" Now at that point, I had no idea what Zig had said to him. I had forgotten. So I said, "What was that, Patrick?" He said, "Dad, you can be whatever you want to be, do whatever you want to do, go wherever you want to go, and have whatever you want to have, as long as you believe in yourself." I said, "Do you believe that, Patrick?" He said, "Sure Dad, don't *you*?" And I had to admit that at that very moment, I didn't. I had forgotten to believe in myself. Yet, I was reminded by a six year old that if I was going to be successful, then I needed to believe in myself. At that moment, my life changed forever.

What about you?

How are *you* doing? Do you believe in yourself? Or have you forgotten to? Stop right now and re-read the words of Zig Ziglar. Believe them as Patrick did. Say them to yourself right now.

I can be whatever I want to be,
I can do whatever I want to do,
I can go wherever I want to go,
I can have whatever I want to have,
as long as I believe in myself !

Believe in abundance.

It is important to recall that it is not really for lack of abundance that you are experiencing want, but for lack of awareness of the ever-present reality of divine substance, and the faith to shape it into manifest form.

Eric Butterworth

The absolute truth is, there is no lack anywhere, but an overflowing abundance of every kind of good which man can possibly desire or conceive of.

H. Emily Cady

Clearly, you will never get into harmony with prosperity, if you insist upon holding images of lack and limitation in the storehouse of your marvelous mind.

Bob Proctor

Abundance reigns everywhere. The only limits we have are those that we encourage with our beliefs in those limits.

Dr. Wayne Dyer

Daily become still, and think about the rich, unlimited substance of the universe that is everywhere present for you to form as prosperous ideas, which will produce prosperous results.

Catherine Ponder

There is enough in the world for everyone to have plenty to live on happily and to be at peace with his neighbors.

Harry S. Truman

Life is synonymous with abundance. Nature is the lavish expression of a Mind which knows no limitation. Creative Intelligence is free from restriction and does not withhold anything from its creations.

Donald Curtis

The belief that there is not enough Good to go around makes it difficult, if not impossible, for Good to be experienced by the one who entertains such a belief.

Ernest Holmes

Do you believe that there is plenty to go around for everyone? Not just plenty, but more than enough? Or are you stuck in the realm of thinking that says there is just so much out there and I have to get my share or I may do without?

Two states of consciousness.

A prosperity consciousness is based on the knowledge that the Universe has provided more than enough food for everyone, more than enough love for everyone, more than enough money for everyone; in fact, more than enough of every good thing for everyone! The reason that people don't have enough and are currently doing without is because they don't believe in abundance and plenty. They have a poverty consciousness.

A poverty consciousness is based on a belief system of lack and limitation. It is based on the thought that supply is limited. This simply isn't so! Stop believing this way. Stop fearing lack. Stop being afraid of being broke. When you fear something, you give it the power to hurt you.

> When you are afraid of something,
> you give it the power to hurt you.

An example of fear in action.

The first time I was in New York City, a friend and I were out on the streets very late doing the tourist thing and gawking at the buildings and the people and the strange stuff going on around us. At the end of one street, a police officer approached us and suggested that we go back to our hotel room. When we asked him why, he told us that it was obvious that we were from out of town. He said that we looked scared and were an easy target for a mugging. I confirmed that we were indeed a bit fearful based on the people and surroundings, but that there were just so many other people around that surely we couldn't really be in any danger. I even pointed out a young woman walking ahead of us by herself. That's when he said, "But look at her. She doesn't look afraid. She walks with confidence. She looks like she knows what she's doing and where she is going. You two don't. You look afraid and fear makes you vulnerable." We recognized what he was telling us was true and went back to our hotel. But what a lesson!

In the Bible, Job said, "The thing I fear has come upon me." In other words, the thing I have believed in has come about. Fear of scarcity and lack is a belief in scarcity and lack. Fear makes us vulnerable to attack. Fearing lack will only bring lack. More clearly: if you are afraid of being broke, your chances of being broke are increased.

Take the advice of the New York City police officer. Walk confidently. Have the appearance that you know where you are going and what you are doing. Look fearless. Act fearless. Be fearless. Reduce your vulnerability.

Take the power away from lack and limitation. Stop believing in them now. Believe in abundance. Believe in *your* abundance!

I am God's gift to the world,
and the world is God's gift to me.

Believe in what you do.

We are not just acted upon by God, but we are the activity of God expressing Himself as us.

Eric Butterworth

I have found that if I have faith in myself and in the idea I am tinkering with, I usually win out.

Charles F. Kettering

In order to be successful at what you do, you must believe in it. Then market your belief. That's what people really want. Your passion. Your belief.

"But do you know what I do?" I don't care what you do. It doesn't matter. If it serves people, then it is honorable and you should believe in it. If you don't believe in it, then quit doing it and do something that you do believe in! It's that simple. Because if you don't believe in what you are doing, then you can't expect anyone else to. And if you don't and they don't, then success will never happen for you!

Believe in others.

No one succeeds alone.

Ray Kroc

No one succeeds alone. You have to have other people. You have to have customers. You need an employer. You need employees and co-workers. You need friends and family. See my point? You need other people. You need support. You need their love. Other people are critical to your success.

And you have to believe in those people. Believe that they are good. Believe that they serve a purpose in your life; that they are there for a reason. Believe that you need them and they need you.

I know that's not always going to be easy. So let me give you a few helpful hints.

Accept people the way they are. They aren't always going to be nice, caring, honest, friendly, or even competent. So have realistic expectations. People are what they are. So don't be judgemental. Don't try to change them. Don't bother trying to figure out why people do the things they do. It will drive you crazy! People are what they are. It's their job. Just accept them and love them in spite of. . .

Believe in the future.

There is a saying, "People change, but not often." While that is true, I want to make it clear that it is not true because people *can't* change. It is true because people *won't* change.

That doesn't have to be the case with you. You can change! Your past is just that: past. It has nothing to do with the present or the future. It never has to be the same for you after this moment. It can be different. In fact, it can be whatever you want it to be.

What kind of future do you want? Think about it. Picture it. Believe that you can have it. Then create it!

> The best way to predict the future
> is to create it.

Believe in a Higher Power.

But seek first the kingdom of God and His righteousness, and all these things shall be added to you.

                                        Matthew 6:33

The person who has a firm trust in the Supreme Being is powerful in his power, wise by his wisdom, happy by his happiness.

Joseph Addison

Without divine assistance I can not succeed; with it I can not fail.

Abraham Lincoln

What we need to realize above all else is that God has provided for the most minute needs of our daily life.

Charles Fillmore

However renumerative our work or investments may be, it is wise to remember that the source of every good thing is God, the Universal Presence.

Margaret R. Stortz

So what does God have to do with this? Only everything. Got a problem with that idea? I know that some people do. That's really too bad. There is no way around it. There is simply no way to talk about money and prosperity without talking about God. (By the way, if you have a problem with the word God, then use another word. Use Higher Consciousness, Infinite Intelligence, Divine Mind, Loving Father/Mother, Divine Love, Universal Mind, Higher Power, or use Elmer! What you call It isn't nearly as important as your belief in It and reliance on It.)

Prosperity is the most spiritual concept I have discovered. However, prosperity has little to do with religion. You won't get this stuff in most churches. Some, but not most. Somehow, most traditional churches have come to believe that there is something Holy about poverty. There isn't. There is nothing holy, spiritual, or, in my opinion even religious, about not having money or any other good thing. So find a church that encourages you to experience *all* of God's good stuff: health, success, happiness, *and* prosperity.

I know that God is a loving God who wants only the best for his
finest creation . . . **me!**

> And you shall remember the Lord
> your God, for it is He who gives you
> power to get wealth . . .
>
> Deuteronomy 8:18

Spirituality and prosperity.

While money and prosperity have little to do with religion, they
have everything to do with being spiritual. Love is the essence of
prosperity. (I will devote a lot more time to this idea later in the
book.) Love is the spiritual thought and belief system of the
Universe. Love is true spirituality in action.

God is love. Love is service. The more you love, the more you
serve. When your motive is service and love, you are serving God.
God is the spirit of, and at the center of, all good, worthwhile
endeavors. Serving other people with your work and with a motive
of love is spiritual and it serves God.

The more you serve, the more you will be served. The Law says that
when we serve, we will be rewarded. No exceptions. It's a Law!

But what about . . .

"What about Mother Teresa? She has love and she definitely serves
others, yet she doesn't have money." True. But it takes a lot of
money to support the work of Mother Teresa. It is like the story of
the interview with one of Gandhi's followers, when he said, "It
takes a lot of money to keep Gandhi in poverty." Plus, prosperity

is not only money and Mother Teresa's reward is at a plane far above the physical plane of dollars and cents. Besides, if you ask her, I'll bet she would claim to be rich!

Some of you might also be saying, "But look at what I do, how can this be loving service to God and mankind?" I don't care whether you are serving hamburgers, sweeping floors, selling auto parts, or anything else. What you do is not important. Your motive, or your reason for doing it is the only thing that is important. Do it for others. Do it with love and to serve others. When you do, you will be serving God.

Don't miss this part!

God wants good things for you. God wants you to have stuff. God wants you to experience every good part of life in the most abundant way. God understands that you must be abundant on the material, physical plane. That's why in the Lord's Prayer, Jesus said, "Give us this day our daily bread." He knew that you have to have your physical needs met in order to deal with the other things in life. You can't think about anything else if you are doing without on the level of food, clothing and shelter. Maslow taught us that in his Hierarchy of Needs. People must be provided for physically before they can deal with their other areas.

Begin now to believe that God wants only the best for you. Believe that God created everything good to be enjoyed by you and that nothing should be withheld from you. Believe that you were created Divinely and deserve the very best of the abundance that is available!

Jesus said in Mark 11:24, "Therefore I say to you, whatever things you ask when you pray, believe that you receive them, and you will have them." Notice that Jesus didn't say, "whatever things you ask for except for money, abundance, prosperity, and riches." He just said *whatever*. Jesus didn't exclude anything, so why do we?

*I have come that they may have life, and that they may have it more
abundantly.*

John 10:10

Believe only in good.

*Whatever things are true, whatever things are noble, whatever
things are just, whatever things are pure, whatever things are
lovely, whatever things are of good report, if there is any virtue and
if there is anything praiseworthy - meditate on these things.*

Phillipians 4:8

Everything is good. Really. It may not seem so at the time but I have
certainly found it always to be so in my life.   So stop looking at the
bad things as bad and start believing that they are actually good.
Know that the outcome of every experience is good. You may have
learned a lesson, taken a new action, or become more as a result of
what happened. And any time you learn, take action, or become
more, that's good!

> There is nothing either
> good or bad but
> thinking makes it so.
>
> Shakespeare

What seems to be your "worst" thing will probably turn out to be
your "best" thing. It did for me. At the time, my business failure
and bankruptcy seemed to be anything but good. Yet look at the
good that came out of that. That situation allowed me to learn the
principles of success which turned into a successful speaking career

and series of books, audio and video cassettes. I have been blessed with the opportunity to share my story and the message of hope with thousands of people all around the world. In fact, you wouldn't be reading this book right now if that hadn't happened. So was it a bad thing? Absolutely not!

Every adversity really does hold the seed of its own possibility. So stop thinking of things as bad. Instead look for the good. It's there. It may be covered by a lot of hurt, pain and ugliness, but I can promise you it's there.

This does not mean that you have to see life through rose colored glasses or be a Pollyanna. It also doesn't mean that you have to be happy about everything that happens to you. No one enjoys a disaster and it would be unreasonable and downright stupid to expect it. Negative emotions are natural when seemingly bad things happen. It is natural to feel them. However, it is destructive to live in those emotions.

An important question.

Is believing only in good, living in denial? Absolutely not. Believing only in good is having foresight. It is being able to look past the immediate circumstances and to know there is a lesson to be learned or some other good that will come from this thing. It is believing in the future. It is having faith. It is living in the knowledge that a Loving Universe is taking care of you.

Please pay close attention to this next part!

By acknowledging the bad, or the things that you don't want, you are giving power to them. What you think about and concentrate on, you attract. Do you want poverty, disease, illness, lack, and limitation to have power over you? Do you want these things to be attracted to you? Of course not!

Stop focusing on what you don't want. In fact, stop believing in them at all. Stop believing in duality, that there is both good and bad. Instead, believe in Unity, that things are only good. God is in everything. God is only good. Everything is good. Simplistic thinking? Not at all. In fact, it's anything but simplistic. This is a tough concept to grasp, but when you do it makes total sense and will have a profoundly positive impact on your life and its outcome. Believe only in good and know that everything that happens does so for your good.

About believing.

Saying that you believe isn't enough. Declaring, "I believe, I believe, I believe!" isn't believing. It is wishing that you believed. Belief is a knowledge that you are willing to put into action without question or doubt. It does no good to talk success and practice failure. It does no good to talk prosperity and practice poverty. And it does no good to talk belief and practice unbelief.

Remember how life works. Beliefs - Actions - Results. Don't forget the action. Action will make the difference. When you are ready to act upon your beliefs without any question and with no doubt, then you will be assured that you believe. Only then will results begin to happen.

After all is said and done, more is said than done.

                                                              Unknown

. . . faith without works is dead.

                                                              James 2:26

A belief is valueless if you don't test it and live by it.
                                                    Paramahansa Yogananda

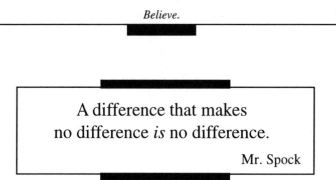

A difference that makes
no difference *is* no difference.

Mr. Spock

CHAPTER

3

Get your attitude right about money.

The word "prosperity" comes from the Latin root which literally translates; "according to hope," or "to go forward hopefully." Thus, it is not so much a condition in life as it is an attitude toward life.

Eric Butterworth

Realize that the only thing that keeps us from the riches that lie all around us is our mental attitude, or the way we look at God, life, and the world in general.

Joseph Murphy

You are rich according to the mental attitudes of your mind which includes the increased expectancy of all things good in your world.

Jack Boland

If you are somehow able to think of yourself as prosperous, and no one or nothing outside of you can deter you from that belief, then in fact your life is a miracle of prosperity.

Dr. Wayne Dyer

Attitude is everything.

We've all heard that one before. And we understand that it's true. We know that looking at things in a positive way greatly impacts what happens in our life. We also understand that being positive is always better than being negative. But did you know that you have an attitude about money? You do. I do. We all do. It's how we think about having it or not having it, or how we use it when we have it, and how we feel about borrowing it, or owing it, or about credit. The list goes on and on. You probably got yours from your parents and they got theirs from their parents. It has been influenced by your social conditions, your ethnic background, your geographic area, your education, your age, and significant and sometimes not so seemingly significant events that all go together to become your personal historical experience in handling money. It is sometimes called the prosperity consciousness or a poverty consciousness which were both mentioned earlier. But call it what you like, you've got one. And it is that attitude that has determined how much money you have in your pocket at this very moment.

If your attitude is based on a belief system that says "money is the root of all evil," then you probably don't have much money. If your attitude is that you don't do something very important in life that's worth very much, you probably don't have much money. If you think that there's just so much money to go around, then you probably aren't going to get much money. If you say things like, "I'll probably always be broke," then you probably always will.

However, if you realize that money is a wonderful thing to have, a fun thing to give away, a tool to do great things with, and a thing to enjoy, then you probably have plenty of it. If you say things like, "if they can do it, then I can do it!" then you probably either have money or are on your way to getting money. If you believe that there is more than enough money to go around, then you are probably experiencing plenty of money.

There is no virtue in poverty; it is a disease like any other mental disease. If you were physically ill, you would think there was something wrong with you. You would seek help and do something about the condition at once. Likewise, if you do not have money constantly circulating in your life, there is something wrong with you.

Joseph Murphy

Indifference.

Never be indifferent towards money. Indifference is dangerous. You make think that saying something like, "I don't care about money" is a lofty, I'm-above-it-all statement. In reality, it's stupid. If you don't care about money, don't expect money to care about you. What you don't care about has a tendency to slip away from you. Is that what you want to happen to your money?

What's your attitude? I can help you with the answer. Just look at how much money you have. If you are doing without the good stuff in life because you don't have enough money, then your attitude needs to be worked on. It's that simple.

Money attitudes.

So what is the right attitude? I believe that there are four key attitudes that go together to form the correct overall attitude about money. They are:

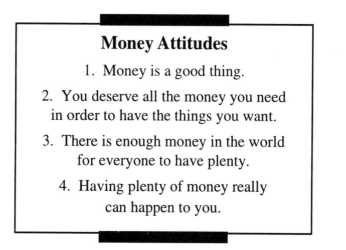

Money Attitudes

1. Money is a good thing.

2. You deserve all the money you need in order to have the things you want.

3. There is enough money in the world for everyone to have plenty.

4. Having plenty of money really can happen to you.

Each of these will be covered throughout the rest of the book. For now, just look at the list of attitudes and accept them to be true as best you can. This may be a real challenge for you. It was for me. I had to throw away nearly forty years of wrong thinking in order to finally get the right attitude about money.

Work on your attitude about money. Come back to this list often until you finally are able to totally accept it and believe it. Even if it takes ten years to get it, you have to get these four attitudes down before you can ever experience abundance, attract riches, and have more money!

CHAPTER

4

Take Responsibility.

We are all self-made; but only the successful will admit it.

Earl Nightingale

When you miss the target, never in history has it been the target's fault.

Unknown

People do not want to take responsibility for the scarcity in their lives. It is much easier to blame circumstances, others, events, or even God for the things that they have failed to acquire or achieve.

Dr. Wayne Dyer

A man's weakness and strength, purity and impurity, are his own, and not another man's; they are brought about by himself, and not by another; and they can only be altered by himself; never by another.

James Allen

If you don't have as much as you would like to have, whose fault is it? Need some help? Let me give you a list to peruse:

the government	my boss	my husband
the economy	my employees	my wife
the system	my customers	my ex-husband
my geographic location	my co-workers	my ex-wife
my environment	my ethnic origin	my children
the politicians	my church	my parents
my education	my religion	my in-laws
the weather	the company	my family

Pretty good list, right? I'll bet you considered at least some of these didn't you? Well, you know by now that if you picked anything from this list, you are wrong. The reason you have what you have, whether it is terrific or terrible, whether you are rich or poor, is you. That makes for a very short list!

It was *your* thinking, *your* beliefs, and *your* actions, that brought you these results. And if you have been spending any time at all blaming someone else then you have been delaying your prosperity.

When my business failed, I put together a sizeable list of people and circumstances to blame. I wasted a lot of time and energy blaming others for what I should have taken responsibility for. It wasn't until I quit blaming others and forgave them and took responsibility and forgave myself that I was finally able to move forward to my greater good. (Forgiveness is an important part of this process and will be dealt with.)

Take responsibility now for your success. Know that your prosperity is your responsibility. Stop laying blame. Stop slowing down your riches.

Life is a banquet.

I love food. I love the way it smells, the way it tastes, and the way it looks. I love to go home to Momma's on holidays and see all the food laid out. I love to go to really good cafeterias and walk past all the beautiful food. I like to see big platters of all kinds of meats, and huge spreads of salads and vegetables, and especially desserts: chocolate desserts! Get the picture?

That's how I see life. Life is like a beautiful banquet. It's the ultimate smorgasbord. It's like the world's best cafeteria with an endless supply of wonderful food. A bounteous feast that never runs out.

However . . .

Life is not like a restaurant; they don't bring it to you. Life is a buffet; you have to serve yourself.

The sad thing is that most people just don't get it. They sit quietly in their seats and watch all the other people getting all the good stuff while they starve to death.

Some will even scream and yell for a waiter to bring them stuff and whine when they don't get it.

Some will get indignant and think that they are too good to get up and wait on themselves.

Some will blame others for getting the best stuff and leaving them the scraps from the bottom of the platter. Some will even blame the restaurant for having such a stupid policy.

All of them will do without. Until they take responsibility and take action, they will starve.

Are you waiting to be served? Forget it. It won't happen. Take responsibility now. Your prosperity is up to you!

Life is a banquet, darling, and most poor people are starving to death.

                                                         Auntie Mame

> Life is not a restaurant;
> they don't bring it to you.
> Life is a buffet;
> you have to serve yourself.

CHAPTER

5

Accept your good.

As you diligently work to think the positive thought, speak the constructive word, and hold the creative success-images in mind, your whole life will begin to vibrate with the dynamic power of prosperity. The law is, you can have all you expect and accept.

Eric Butterworth

You are whole, complete, and your success in life will be in direct proportion to your ability to accept this truth about you.

Dr. Robert Anthony

Wealth is attracted to the person who is emotionally and intellectually ready to accept it, expect it, and enjoy it.

Jerry Gillies

We never have to convince God of our need, but rather we have to convince ourselves that God has already provided for our good.

Florence Scovel Shinn

Whoever lifts his cup of acceptance to the outpouring of the Divine abundance shall find that it will be filled.

Ernest Holmes

To have abundance in our lives requires a willingness to recognize that it is always available; we need only open ourselves to receive it.

Arnold Patent

Do you understand how good you are? Do you know that you were created perfect and are still perfect? The imperfections that you see are based on your limited understanding of your good. These imperfections are not real and therefore mean nothing. Stop believing in them and they will cease to exist.

Instead, know that you are divinely created and full of good. You are the physical manifestation of the hands of God. You are the expression of Love in the Universe. Begin now to accept this about yourself.

*Man travels hundreds of miles to gaze at the broad expanse of the
ocean, he looks into the heavens with amazement . . . he gazes at the
rivers and fields and streams in awe, and then passes himself by
without a thought . . . the most amazing creation of all.*

St. Augustine (Paraphrased)

How are you doing?

How are you at accepting your own good? Are you surprised when
people do good things for you? What about when people say nice
things about you and pay you compliments? Surprised? Why?
How can you be surprised when someone wants to do good for you
when you are a Divine creation of all good?

As a perfect creation people will want to do you good. In fact, you
should expect people to do you good by knowing that you deserve
only the best from life.

Reverse Paranoia.

Become a "reverse paranoid." A reverse paranoid is a person who
believes that the whole world is plotting to do them good. (And it
really is!) We need to understand that everything that happens,
whether seemingly good or bad at the time, really does hold the seed
of infinite possibility.

Start now to practice accepting your good. Begin by saying thank
you for the good that is you. Say thank you for the good things you
already have, knowing that you deserve them. Learn to accept
compliments. Compliments are gifts and should be accepted
willingly and gratefully. Allow people to do you good. Graciously
accept gifts from others whether given in word, deed or form.

A different twist.

By accepting gifts from others you are playing a role in their expression of good. You are allowing them to give and become a part of the Law of Sowing and Reaping. By not accepting any gift, you are interrupting that Law and you rob then of their ability to participate in their expression of good.

There is always the perfect balance of giving and receiving, and though man should always give without thinking of returns, he violates law if he does not accept the returns which come to him; for all gifts are from God, man being merely the channel.
                                        Florence Scovel Shinn

Say no to your gifts, and soon there won't be any.
                                        Mike Wickett

> If you lack any good thing, you are still asleep to your own good.
> Florence Scovel Shinn

Increase your deservability.

Man was born to be rich or inevitably to grow rich through the use of his faculties.
                                        Ralph Waldo Emerson

God is not willing for you to settle for anything less than everything.
                                        Jack Boland

By learning to accept your good, you will come to understand that you deserve good things. You deserve the best. You deserve every good thing that exists. You deserve money, love, a beautiful home, a great car, and wonderful relationships. You deserve it all!

> You can have just as much money
> as you believe you deserve.

Whenever any thought of lack enters your mind it is the result of a belief that you deserve less than the best. That simply isn't so. Stop yourself at that very instant and repeat the words, "I deserve only the best." Refuse to accept less than the best for yourself. Turn away from mediocrity in your life. Refuse to believe that you deserve less than everything.

Relax.

Acceptance does not imply effort even though "learning to accept" may take effort. So relax. Expect abundance. Believe abundance. Know that you deserve wealth and riches and good things of every type. Stop chasing your greater good. You already have it. Accept it. Enjoy it!

Caution!

Don't think that to relax means to be lazy. It doesn't. I mean relax in consciousness. In other words, don't fret or worry. Your good is there; relax.

When we learn to trust the
Universe, we shall be happy,
prosperous and well.

Ernest Holmes

Talk to yourself right.

So shall my word be that goes forth from my mouth: it shall not return to me void, but it shall accomplish what I please, and it shall prosper in the thing for which I sent it.

Isaiah 55:11

For by your words you will be justified, and by your words you will be condemned.

Matthew 12:37

Words are the most powerful drug used by mankind.

Rudyard Kipling

Your words are the outpicturing of your consciousness. If you want to know what you really believe, listen to your words. Nothing can change until your words change.

Jack Boland

Death and life are in the power of the tongue . . .

Proverbs 18:21

Your words are powerful. They act as magnets to bring to you that which you talk about.

When I was still in the telecommunications business, I reached a point where I really didn't enjoy what I was doing. In fact, I hated it. I dreaded having to get up to go to the office. I got to the point where I despised the industry as a whole. I didn't really enjoy any part of the business. I used to drag myself out of bed in the morning and say, "I would give anything not to have to do this any more." The Universe heard me. I didn't just give anything, I gave everything. The business failed and I lost everything. Did my words bring that about? Yes. I talked about it and as a result, focused on it and made it happen in my experience.

There is an old saying, "Be careful what you ask for, you just might get it." Take that another step. Be careful what you say, even jokingly; it will probably come to pass!

> ## What you think about and
> ## talk about, comes about!

Good advice.

Florence Scovel Shinn once wrote that our words should only be used for three purposes, "to heal, to bless, and to prosper." Think of the impact that each of us could have on everyone we come in contact with if we would just follow that sound advice. Do it just for a week. Stop criticizing, complaining, griping, gossiping and putting yourself and other people, circumstances and situations down. The results will be amazing!

Speak in terms of your blessings rather than in terms of your challenges.

Catherine Ponder

A new meaning.

Look up the word "bless" in your dictionary. You will find that one of the meanings of this little word is "to confer prosperity upon." Think about that one. So start blessing. Bless yourself. Bless your stuff. Bless your friends. Bless everything. Bless me . . . please!

What you bless you multiply. What you condemn you lose.

Joseph Murphy

The next step.

Never speak negatively about anything you have or about any condition that exists. Speaking negatively about it or condemning it in any way shows that you are ungrateful. Ungratefulness in any form, whether in thought or word, will only cause that condition to multiply and slow down your prosperity.

Talk differently about money.

Listen to the way you talk about money. Most of us grow up hearing what a dirty, filthy thing money is.

I'm going to give you a list of things that you have probably heard and maybe even said about money. If this list is at all familiar, stop saying these things. This list will keep you broke.

Money is dirty (filthy rich.)
It takes money to make money.
Money is the root of all evil.
You can't take it with you.
The best things in life are free.
Money isn't everything.
Money doesn't grow on trees.
Save for a rainy day.
A penny saved is a penny earned.
Money can't buy you love.
There are people starving in China.
What if something terrible happens? (and all the other "what if's")

With my luck.

People who say "with my luck" almost always follow it with something terrible. "With my luck, I'll work here the rest of my life!" "With my luck, I'll never have anything really nice!" "With

my luck, I'll drive this old thing until the wheels fall off!" Stop!
Only say "with my luck" if you are going to follow it with something
terrific!

I can't afford it.

Never say "I can't afford it." As long as you are saying what you
can't afford, you will never be able to afford it. If you must say
anything, say "I don't choose to use the money I have to buy that at
this time." This is a declaration that you indeed have money (and
you do) and a statement that you are exercising your power of choice
to spend it as you choose. That is a statement of your power, not
your weakness.

A sad story.

I was parking my car at a mall recently, when a family came along
behind me on their way into the mall. The mother turned to her
husband and three children and said, "Get one thing straight, we
can't afford anything in there and never will be able to, so there is
no reason to even waste your time wanting anything!" Think of the
damage that well-meaning mother caused herself, her husband and
her children. Damage that they may never be able to break away
from. I wanted to grab those little kids and say, "No, that's not true,
you can have anything here that you want, maybe not today, but
there's no reason you can't have it all someday, and until then it's
great to spend your time wanting it!"

Great stuff from Larry's shower wall:

I want to share something very private with you. It is my own
personal prosperity affirmation. It is laminated and hanging on the
wall of my shower. It's on my shower wall so I can start every

morning with it. It has worked for me and I'll guarantee that if you
will say it with belief it will work for you too!

My world is abundant! I am rich and
getting richer! I have more than enough
money to pay for anything I want, any
time I want it. My pocket is always full
of money. My checking account always
has more than enough to pay all of my
obligations. I have more than I need and
all that I want. I have surplus money! I
expect abundance and success, therefore I
get abundance and success. Money
comes at me from all directions! Everywhere I turn, there are people there to do
me good. My mail and my telephone
bring me good news and great wealth.
My calendar is always full of profitable,
fun, exciting opportunities! I speak words
of love and wisdom. I serve others. I am
ready for opportunities to do good for
others. I give freely and lovingly of all
that I have. I am always thankful!

You do it.

Write your own prosperity affirmation. Write several. Put the quotes in this book on 3 X 5 cards and carry them around with you. Bombard your mind with the pure, the powerful, the positive and the prosperous. Post them wherever you will see them. The shower is a great place. So is the dashboard of your car. Use them as book marks. Read them, memorize them and meditate on them. Form the habit of thinking positively about your money and only saying things that confirm the level of prosperity you really want.

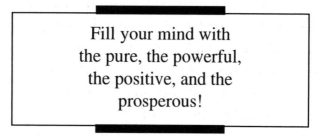

Fill your mind with
the pure, the powerful,
the positive, and the
prosperous!

Picture prosperity.

. . . whatever exists as a mental picture in Mind must tend to, and finally does take form if the picture is really believed in and embodied.

Ernest Holmes

If you want to experience prosperity at a miraculous level, you must leave behind your old ways of thinking and develop a new way of imagining what is possible for you to experience in your life.

Dr. Wayne Dyer

Man, himself, limits his supply by his limited vision.

Florence Scovel Shinn

Faith is to believe what we do not see; and the reward of this faith is to see what we believe.

St. Augustine

Daily we must train our thoughts to see only that which we wish to experience; and since we are growing into what we are mentally dwelling upon, we should put all small and insignificant thoughts and ideals out of our thinking and see things in a larger way.

Ernest Holmes

Visualization and my prosperity.

A few years ago, at a convention of the National Speakers Association, I was talking with my friend and mentor, Joe Charbonneau. We were attending a reception being held in the main room where all the general sessions were being conducted. The room had a stage, beautiful backdrop; the works. Joe told me to go up on the stage and look out at the room and picture myself being a general session speaker. He said to visualize the crowd, the applause, and to see myself standing there in front of them. I wasn't really comfortable going up on the stage with all those people standing around at the reception, but Joe insisted. I had only been a member of the association for less than two years and I knew that my getting to address the group at a general session was many years away. I knew that you had to be a big dog to be asked to speak to the entire association. But, I did it anyway. I walked up on the stage, looked out at that room, closed my eyes and visualized myself giving the speech of my life. I heard the applause, I saw the standing ovation, and I felt the success! (And no one in the room that night even noticed me up there.)

Six months later, I *was* standing up there on that stage giving my speech at a general session of the National Speakers Association. The applause was there, the feeling of success was there, even the standing ovation was there. Only two years as a professional speaker and there I was! People told me how lucky I was to pull that off. I know that it had nothing to do with luck. I know that it was because I was willing to listen to my mentor, who believed in me more than I did at that moment. Then, I acted on that belief. I visualized it happening. I removed all doubts about it happening. I suspended all disbelief. I became willing to accept my good. I believed it could happen. And it came to pass!

That single act of visualization has been one of my most prosperous acts. It got me noticed by other speakers and by speakers bureaus who would never have taken a chance on a new guy like me. It gave me confidence. It opened a whole new market for me as a humorist. It brought me more bookings, more credibility, more notoriety, more acknowledgment, and more money than I could have gotten in five years "the hard way."

> Whatever you vividly imagine,
> ardently desire, sincerely believe,
> and enthusiastically act upon must
> inevitably come to pass.
>
> Paul J. Meyer

Is there something you want to be, do, or have? Then visualize yourself being, doing or having it. Close your eyes and *see* it. Picture it clearly.

Negative visualization.

You have a vision right now for your life whether you have consciously realized it or not. You have pictured the things you want to happen. Hopefully, your visualization has been positive. However, that is not usually the case. Most visualization is negative. Most people picture what they don't want to happen instead of what they do. It is called " worry." Worry is the misuse and abuse of your imagination. Nearly 100% of what you worry about never happens. Therefore, worry is a complete waste of your time. It will do nothing but slow down the flow of money into your life.

The worst thing that could happen rarely happens. Stop expecting it. Stop picturing it. Start now to picture what you do want to happen. Picture only the best for yourself. See money flowing to you in unexpected ways. Visualize a bank account with lots of money. Picture the car you want and the home you want and see yourself in the picture.

You must see it first in your mind if you are ever going to see it in your reality.

However ...

Visualization of money does not mean that you are going to wake up and suddenly have a bank account that's full of money. It doesn't mean that when you step out of your house to get in your car, that there will be a new one where the old one once was. And when you wake up in the morning, don't expect for your bed to have magically reappeared in the house of your dreams. When you visualize the money, the car, the house or anything else, you have visualized the end result. That is important and there is certainly nothing wrong with it, but you have left out the most important step.

The Real Key To Visualization

The most important thing to visualize is the contribution you will be making. Without the contribution, you won't get the reward. Visualize yourself doing the service that will ultimately be rewarded with the money. See yourself performing a service that you love, and see other people benefiting from that service. Then the money will be automatic.

CHAPTER

8

Do what you love and the money will come.

If one advances confidently in the direction of his own dreams, and endeavors to live the life which he has imagined, he will meet with a success unexpected in common hours.

Thoreau

It's valuable to understand that the loving energy you put into your work is what provides you with a large income.

Jerry Gillies

The happiness we feel when we do what we love is a gift we give to ourselves.

Arnold Patent

Do what you love. Do what makes your heart sing, and never do it for the money. Seek ye first the kingdom of Heaven, and the Masaratti will get here when it's supposed to.

Marianne Williamson

You are not put here to make a living, but to live your making and by living your making, to make your living.

Les Brown

I slept and dreamt that life was joy. I awoke and saw that life was duty. I acted, and behold, duty was joy.

Rabindranath Tagore

You've achieved success in your field when you don't know whether what you're doing is work or play.

Warren Beatty

Follow your bliss.

Joseph Campbell

Ask yourself the question, "What would I do if I could do anything in the world and money was no consideration?" Are you doing that for a living now? Why not? What's holding you back? Fear of being broke?

Ask yourself the motive you have for doing what you are doing right now. If it's for the money, the prestige, or if you are doing it for your family, then it's for the wrong reasons. Doing it may give you plenty of money and prestige, and there is nothing wrong with money and prestige, but the motive is still wrong. And I doubt you will reach your full level of possible prosperity if you are doing it for any reason other than love. You must love what you do in order to achieve your highest and purest level of service, and to achieve ultimate prosperity.

"But what I love doesn't pay well!"

This gives you two options. First, try to fall in love with what you are already doing. Look at it again from a different perspective. See the service you are providing. See the good that people receive from the work that you do. Look at what attracted you to the job in the first place. Remember when it was new and exciting. Make a list of all the good things about your current employment. Write down everything you can think of. If you are totally honest with yourself, then I'll bet that you find plenty of good things. Stop looking at all of the negatives and start focusing on the positives. Fall in love with the good things.

The second option is to quit doing what you don't love and to start doing what you do love. This option is sometimes scary. It is stepping out onto the skinny limbs in faith. However, a complete trust in the Universe and your abilities will help you. If you are a responsible person who has always paid your bills and provided for your family doing one thing, then you will be just as responsible doing another thing. You won't change just because your vocation does.

> Life is an opportunity for you to
> contribute love in your own way.
> Bernie Siegel, M. D.

A word of warning.

Don't automatically quit your job and take up fishing for a living. First, try to fall in love with what you are currently doing. Or, fall in love with the people you are doing it for or with the benefits they get from it. If that doesn't work, then look at what you are passionate about. Explore all of the ways that other people make a living in that field. Find a mentor. Get really good at it before you rely on it as your sole support. Then take the necessary steps to do it for a living.

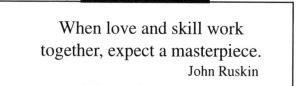

> When love and skill work
> together, expect a masterpiece.
> John Ruskin

The Sunday Night Blues.

While we are not always sure what we want to do, we are always sure what we don't want to do. Did you ever get a sick feeling in the pit of your stomach, or maybe a headache on Sunday night because you knew you had to get up and go to work on Monday morning? Or maybe you just got "down in the dumps" with worry and frustration. I call this the Sunday Night Blues. I used to get them every Sunday night. Consequently, everything in my life suffered:

my health, my peace of mind, my business and my family. As a result, my business failed. How fortunate for me that was all that I lost. I kept my health, my family, and I regained my peace of mind. I was released to do what I love to do. All I lost was dollars. I could always get more dollars. The other things are priceless.

Hating what you do for a living is a miserable way to live your life. Don't do it. Refuse to be unhappy. It is your choice. Choose to live a life of fulfillment. This can only be done by loving what you do and doing what you love.

I encourage you to embrace one of my personal philosophies: *"When it quits being fun, quit!"*

> When you and I are willing to trust
> the Higher Laws, when we are willing
> to go and do what we love to do in
> service of other people, we will get so
> much support, the abundance will
> be so phenomenal we will have to shove
> it away to keep it from coming in.
>
> Mike Wickett

Stop working hard.

The prosperous life is not a struggle. It is the easier, softer, more beautiful, acceptable way.

Jack Boland

Probably the most difficult thing we've got to overcome on planet earth is the old idea that says, "If you're going to be successful you've got to work hard."

Mike Wickett

Been working hard? Are you rich yet? Why not? I'll bet that you always heard that hard work was the key to "making it." Well, it isn't! Most people work hard all of their lives and still end up broke. Studies tell us that at the age of retirement, only one percent of our society ends up rich while eighty per cent end up on Social Security as their sole source of income. Does that mean that the eighty per cent didn't work hard? I don't think so. It means that working hard will make you tired but it won't necessarily make you rich.

Work hard - Play hard. That is an idea based in separation. The two must go together. In fact, it should really just be "play hard." If you interviewed the people in the world who are making big bucks, I bet they would tell you that they are having a ball.

This is not to say that you should be lazy. It is only to say that when you love what you do, the work won't seem like work. It will look like work - hard work. But you'll be having fun!

Other stupid sayings.

No pain, No gain. I'll bet you've heard that one! It's not true! Stop believing that. It only has to be that way if you make the decision that it has to be that way. If you sincerely believe that you must experience pain before you can reap the reward, then get ready for the pain. Your belief will make it a reality for you.

Work is the price you pay for money. No! It doesn't have to be that way. Money will come to you in much simpler ways than by hard work. In fact, you should begin now to re-word that statement as, "Love is the gift you give for money!"

Opportunity comes disguised as hard work. One more time, hard work never made any body rich. Opportunity will make you rich, but only if you seize it! Opportunities are everywhere. Become observant, learn to recognize them, and take advantage of them.

Opportunities are never missing, but we often miss opportunities.
Lloyd Ogilvie

It is better to be prepared for an opportunity and not have one, than to have an opportunity and not be prepared.
Whitney Brown

The harder you work, the luckier you get. Forget luck. Everything that happens to you does so for a reason. For every effect, there has been a cause. Stop expecting luck. As Jim Rohn says, "Things don't just happen, they happen just . . ."

One more time.

If you want to really be rich, either do what you love or fall in love with what you are doing. You will enjoy it more, be better at it, and be paid more for it.

> If we just do what we love, love what we do, and express ourselves fully and freely, we are serving others in accordance to our purpose. All that is left is for us to open ourselves to receive.
>
> Arnold Patent

CHAPTER

9

Stop competing.

If you continue to put your energy into competing with others to avoid loss, you will continue to lose. If you put your energy into stopping another, you are the one who will be stopped. When you concentrate on competing, you stop your own prosperity and creative expansion because you put aside your own individual goals and purposes.

Terry Cole-Whittaker

That old law about "an eye for an eye" leaves everybody blind.
Martin Luther King Jr.

When you win at the expense of someone else, you do not win - you lose.

Larry Winget

The quickest way to cause wealth to take wings and fly away is to criticize and condemn others who have more than you.
John Randolph Price

When we see lack instead of abundance, we immediately create for ourselves a win-lose context.

Terry Cole-Whittaker

I don't believe in competing. In fact, I have abandoned the whole concept of competition. Competition says that only one prize is available and we must all compete to get it. To compete means that someone has to win and someone has to lose. It may be that way in sports, but not in life. This kind of thinking is based on a belief system of scarcity and lack. It reinforces the thought that there is not enough good to go around.

> Competition is based on
> a belief system of scarcity and lack.

Competition encourages comparison.

Competition implies that you have a competitor with the same attributes as you have - two equals fighting it out. Not true. No one has to offer what you have to offer. So to compare yourself to someone else is ridiculous. The only comparison necessary in business is to compare yourself to what the customer needs, not to what the other guy has. The only comparison necessary in life is to compare yourself against what you have the potential of being.

Celebrate the successes of others.

Rejoice and be glad in the progression, advancement, and prosperity of all men. Whatever you claim as true for yourself, claim it for all men everywhere. Do not ever try to deprive another of any joy.
Joseph Murphy

When someone in the same business as you experiences a success, celebrate their success, even when they were chosen instead of you.

"Celebrate their success?" Absolutely. Be glad for them. This is tough, I know. Especially when you know things about them that the customer doesn't know. Things like the fact that they have lousy service, or offer an inferior product, or are on the verge of going out of business. Even when that is the case, you must still be glad for them.

I'm not saying that you have to be happy that you didn't get the business. I am only saying that you shouldn't worry about the fact that you didn't get *this* piece of business. There is plenty of business out there - more than enough for every one.

You can't lose what you don't have.

In business, we often say that we "lost" a particular piece of business. That is impossible. If it was new business that you were pursuing, then you didn't have it to begin with. If you didn't have it to begin with, how could you lose it?

If it was existing business, and it goes away to do business with someone else, then again, I contend that you didn't really ever have it. They might have bought from you before, but you didn't really *have* their business. You had only *done* business with them.

Let it go, it will come back.

When customers "make a mistake" by choosing someone else, then it won't take them long to recognize it. At that point, the business usually comes to you with much greater enthusiasm on their part and much less effort to obtain it on your part.

My personal experience has shown me that whenever I release a piece of business and am sincerely happy for everyone involved, that the business I didn't get that time is usually returned to me many times over.

The solution.

Operate from a belief system of abundance. No one is getting your piece of the pie. When another business or person does a good job, then the pie only gets bigger for everyone.

Wish for others exactly what you would wish for yourself. Bless (confer prosperity upon) them. Want them to do well. Rejoice in their successes.

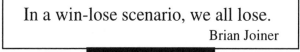

In a win-lose scenario, we all lose.
Brian Joiner

CHAPTER

10

*Money will
come to you
as it goes
<u>from</u> you.*

. . . for whatever a man sows, that he will also reap.

Galations 6:7

Therefore, whatever you want men to do to you, do also to them . . .

Matthew 7:12

As you have done, it shall be done to you . . .

Obadiah 1:15

How does money go from you?

Do you tithe, pay your bills or pay your taxes grudgingly? Then that is how money will come to you: grudgingly. Do you drag out paying your bills to the last minute just because you know you can get by with it? Then don't be surprised when you are paid in the same manner for the services you render.

Pay your bills happily.

When you get a bill, pay it with a smile. Don't gripe about it. Don't complain when the mail carrier brings you the mail and all you see is bills. Be glad that you are a prosperous person and that you have plenty of money to pay them. Affirm it and it will become true.

It also helps to remember why you got that bill. When the electric bill comes, give thanks for the electricity you enjoyed. When the car payment is due, bless the car you drive for getting you to all of those places you needed and wanted to go. Give thanks for the service or the product you enjoyed that generated the bill in the first place.

Paying your bills gladly will set a Law in motion that will cause others to happily pay for the product and service you provide.

Pay your taxes enthusiastically.

Have I gone too far? It may seem hard to enthusiastically pay your taxes, but I'll bet you enthusiastically enjoy the benefits those taxes pay for - the streets, the police protection, the firefighters, the freedom. It's easy to complain about the government and all of the waste that is prevalent in so many areas. Jim Rohn says that of course government is fat and lazy, but aren't we all a little overweight and a bit lazy?

You earned the money that the taxes must be paid on. You enjoyed the money, didn't you? When you are paying taxes, it means you have made money. The more you make, the more you pay. When you don't have any taxes to pay, there is a very good chance that you are broke. I had a year that I paid no taxes. No taxes, can you imagine? I never want that again. Because that year, I made no money! I was broke! Believe me, it's easier to pay taxes on the money you have, than to pay no taxes on the money you don't have.

> It is easier to pay taxes
> on the money you have,
> than to pay no taxes on
> the money you don't have!

How credit works.

Credit is judged on two things: willingness to pay and ability to pay. While you may not be high on ability, you can always be high on willingness. You must demonstrate this willingness by paying regularly.

What To Do When You Are Behind

• Take responsibility for the debt. Don't waste anyone's time with excuses. The bottom line is that you are behind and it is your own fault. No one wants to hear you whine and moan about all the bad stuff that caused you to fall behind. Own up to your responsibilities. Admit that the debt is yours and that you intend to take care of it.

• Be friendly with your creditors. It only hurts you to become antagonistic. The people who contact you regarding your account are only doing their job and have nothing against you personally. The reason you are angry with them in the first place is because you are embarrassed. You have fallen behind and are now being held accountable and are being forced to face up to your responsibilities. This isn't the creditor's fault. It's yours. So don't take your embarrassment out on them. Regardless of what they might say, stay calm.

• Communicate with your creditors. A lack of communication will make your creditors nervous. Talk to them. Ignore them or dodge their telephone calls and they will lose their trust in you, your willingness and ability.

• Write your creditors a letter. Tell them that you understand about willingness and ability. Advise them that from this moment on, you are going to demonstrate your willingness by sending a payment every month. While you may have already done this through a conversation, demonstrate that you are willing to commit in writing. You may even want to send something every week, depending on the type of account and the amount owed. How much you send is not nearly as important as the fact that you are sending something. Enclose a payment with your letter. At least something. I have made $5 payments on $25,000 debts.

• Negotiate payments at the highest level possible. The people who call you or write to you are usually not at the level where they are able to negotiate. They are following guidelines, policies and procedures. They won't know how to handle a person who is responding with Love and concern for correcting the situation. Most won't understand a partial repayment plan. If the person you are speaking with tells you that they are not allowed to accept partial payments, then insist on speaking to their supervisor. If the supervisor won't accept the partial payment, then ask for their manager. Keep going up until you find someone who will accept your plan. I have found that there is someone in every organization willing to take your money. Keep asking *nicely* until you find that person.

- As your ability to pay increases (and it will) send more. Over-deliver on your promises. You will be amazed at the impact this action will have on your creditors. The creditor's number one goal is to have your bill paid. Every reduction in the outstanding debt is progress toward that end. As long as you show progress everyone will be happy.

- Never lie. Never do anything to destroy the trust that you are working to rebuild. If you don't have the money, tell them the truth. Send what you do have. Always do what you say you are going to do when you said you would do it. Always!

- Remember the Hole Principle - When You Find Yourself In One, Stop Digging! Don't increase your indebtedness. Don't try to borrow yourself out of debt. While there is nothing wrong with credit and with borrowing, there is no excuse for abusing it.

- See the bill paid. Visualize yourself out of debt and prosperous. Refuse to think of yourself as a person who is always struggling with debt and never able to get ahead. Look at the bills in front of you and see the amount owed as $0.00! Hold this picture in your mind until it becomes a reality.

It works both ways.

There will be times when you are the creditor. Remember to treat the people who owe you the way you want to be treated as a debtor. Be kind, understanding, loving, and forgiving. Be the kind of creditor who works with people so everyone can win and not against people so only you can win.

Spend.

Almost any man knows how to earn money, but not one in a million knows how to spend it.

Thoreau

Money is like an arm or a leg - use it or lose it.

Henry Ford

Spend your money. Willingly. Freely. Not foolishly! Enjoy sharing the money you have. Of course you should save your money and invest your money. However, you should also learn to spend without fear. Don't think that lack and poverty may be thrust upon you, so you'd better put something away for a rainy day. More money is always on the way.

> Keep your money circulating.
> If you hoard it for a rainy day,
> you may have to spend it on an ark.
>
> John Randolph Price

CHAPTER

11

Be thankful.

When we become lax in the expression of gratitude, we become little people with little minds, leading little, inconsequential lives.

Eric Butterworth

When we hear somebody complaining that he has not enough, we may know that he has not expressed enough appreciation for what he already has.

Lowell Fillmore

The first step toward discarding a scarcity mentality involves giving thanks for everything that you are and everything that you have.

Dr. Wayne Dyer

. . . in everything give thanks . . .

I Thessalonians 5:18

Gratitude is not only the greatest of virtues, but the parent of all the others.

Cicero

Be thankful for what you have.

"But I don't have very much, so what do I have to be thankful for?" What do you mean you have nothing to be thankful for? You are reading this book aren't you? Then you have eyes that see, the ability to read, and you are alive. Three good things right there to be thankful for. See how easy it is? Be thankful for the simple things.

Make a "Thankful For" list.

Get a pad of Post-its and each morning write down five things you are thankful for. Then stick that little note somewhere in front of you all day to remind yourself of all that you have. If you are going to spend most of the day in the car, then stick it on your steering wheel. If you use a calendar, then stick it on today's date. Stick it on your computer, your telephone, your typewriter, or desk. Get it in front of you to establish a consciousness of thankfulness, or an attitude of gratitude.

Be thankful for the job you have, or your health, list the stuff you own, your car and house, write down the names of your family, your knowledge or education, your opportunities, your talents and abilities, friends, happiness, your beliefs, your faith, yourself.

You could have less.

No matter how little you may think you have, you could have less. So don't whine and wallow in your lack. Remember the saying, "I felt sorry for the man who had no shoes, until I saw a man who had no feet." There are lots of people who have it worse than you do. And there are many who have overcome much more terrible odds than yours to reach success.

Things could also be worse for you than they are now. Believe me, if there is one thing it can always get, it's worse! So don't say something stupid like, "Things just couldn't be any worse." That's a challenge you don't want answered.

So even when things seem terrible for you, be thankful. Bless what you have. Remember that you have been given the talent and abilities to become anything you want and that the world is abundant and waiting to give you all that you need.

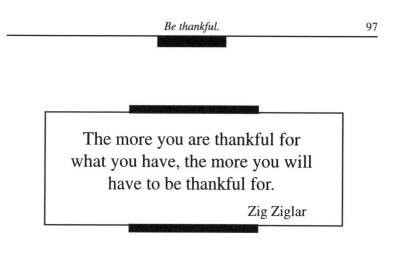

The more you are thankful for
what you have, the more you will
have to be thankful for.

Zig Ziglar

Be thankful for what you are going to have.

Don't just give thanks for what you have right now or for the things
that are happening to you. Give thanks in advance. Give thanks for
things that are going to happen. Say thank you today for what you
are going to have tomorrow. Then believe and act with confidence
as if the thing has already happened.

A simple rule.

Be thankful today for what you are going to have tomorrow, in order
to have today. Be thankful for what you have today, in order to have
tomorrow.

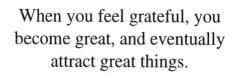

When you feel grateful, you
become great, and eventually
attract great things.

Plato's Law

Ask for help.

. . . you do not have because you do not ask.

James 4:2

And I say to you, ask, and it will be given to you; seek, and you will find; knock, and it will be opened to you. For everyone who asks receives, and he who seeks finds, and to him who knocks it will be opened.

Luke 11: 9, 10

Never ask a poor person how to get rich.

Joseph J. Charbonneau

He who walks with wise men will be wise . . .

Proverbs 13:20

Need help? We all do. Not one of us has all of the information. The good news is there is someone out there who knows what you need to know, someone who is willing to help you.

The very best way to get the help you need is to ask for it. You don't get what you need, want, or deserve; you get what you ask for!

I am amazed at how easy it is to ask for help and get it. I am a seminar junkie. While I speak professionally more than one hundred times a year, I still love to attend seminars and speeches. I enjoy being the recipient of the knowledge and experience of other speakers who are willing to share. At each one of the seminars I attend, a break is usually taken. When that happens, I make a dash for the speaker. I always have at least one question that I need answered. There is rarely a line. All that wealth of knowledge and experience standing right there in the front of the room and no one is taking advantage of it. I can't believe it!

As the speaker, I experience the same thing. Very seldom do I have someone with a burning desire to have their question answered. Why is that? Speakers and teachers love to talk. They love to have people ask them questions. They are paid to be there to share their experience and knowledge. They love what they have to say. So why don't most people take advantage of the situation? It's a mystery!

There are other ways to ask for help. While it's easy to ask someone for a quick word of advice or for help with a specific need, there are other, more formal ways to get help.

The Power of the Master Mind.

In Napoleon Hill's classic book, <u>Think and Grow Rich</u>, he talks about the requirement of power to accumulate money. One of the primary sources of power he discusses is the power of the Master Mind Principle. According to Napoleon Hill:

The "Master Mind" may be defined as: "coordination of knowledge and effort, in a spirit of harmony, between two or more people for the attainment of a definite purpose."

This principle was first brought to Mr. Hill's attention by Andrew Carnegie and was reinforced many times through the hundreds of financially successful people interviewed by Napoleon Hill.

It is really a simple idea that says, "Two heads are better than one." It is based on the principle that when people come together to share their accumulated experience and are willing to openly communicate with each other and support and encourage each other in reaching their dreams, then dreams become reality.

Again, from Napoleon Hill:

When a group of individual brains are coordinated and function in harmony, the increased energy created through that alliance becomes available to every individual brain in the group.

A Master Mind group consists of a group of people who meet regularly in an atmosphere of complete trust. They can be designed around a specific topic or for a specific purpose or they can be for the overall betterment of the individuals. You can be a member of many Master Mind groups. I encourage you put one together soon.

Mentoring

Another form of finding help is through a mentor. This is a person who will take you under their wing and "show you the ropes." It may be a relationship that lasts several years or it could last for just a few minutes. Finding a mentor is not always an easy thing to do. You may never find one through your searching. Instead, be willing for the mentor to find you. "When the student is ready, the teacher will be provided." An ancient proverb that really works! Your ability to find a mentor depends more on you than the mentor. Be a willing student and your mentor will appear.

You may also have mentors that you never meet. I have many. I have been helped, yet have never asked the mentor a question or talked to them in person. How? Through books and tapes. It's a great way to be mentored. (See Chapter 18, "Study Prosperity.")

On the other hand, you will have people who are more than willing to be your mentor. People who are eagerly willing to share their ideas and experiences. Before you jump with both feet into a relationship like this, you need to evaluate the mentor.

Guidelines For Evaluating A Mentor.

• A mentor must be a person who knows what you need to know. A real basic. There are many teachers who haven't a clue. Move on.

• A mentor must be honest and have integrity. There is an old saying, "You can't get a good deal from a bad guy." You can't get good information from a bad guy, either.

- A mentor must be willing to help. Just because they know what you want to know, doesn't mean they are willing to share it. Find out how willing they are to invest in your success.

- A mentor must have a similar belief system. There are many paths. Some are not the kind that you are going to want to take. There are lots of ways to make money. Most of which, I want nothing to do with. Again, it all goes to your motive and belief system.

- A mentor must care about your success. Do they care about you? Do they sincerely want you to become a winner? Or are they entering into this relationship so they can become the winner? A good mentor is there for *you*. They know that the Universe will reward them and aren't concerned about their own success when helping you.

- A mentor must have the time to help you. So many people, so little time. While a mentor may pass in every other category, they may simply not have the time to help you. Don't push them. Be patient. Another mentor will show up who has the time.

- A mentor will be tough on you - tell you the truth without pulling any punches. A mentor who really loves you and wants the best for you will be tough. You aren't looking for agreement, you are looking for help. Listen to your mentor. Be coachable.

- A mentor has perspective. A mentor who has only known success has very little to teach you. You need someone who has been on both sides of the fence. You need a mentor who understands where you have been, where you are, and where you need to go.

Be a mentor.

Those who have bear an obligation to teach and assist others in having ...

Terry Cole-Whittaker

At the moment you discover a truth, even a small one, you are obligated to share it. Not to share it is to steal from those who could use the information and benefit from it. Not sharing it also robs you of the joy you will feel from sharing it. It will also block the flow of good into your life. To keep the good coming in, you must keep it flowing. Give away what you know.

Need to know vs. want to know.

Right now, you know something that someone else wants to know. I didn't say *needs* to know. I said *wants* to know. There is a big difference. Don't bother with those who need to know. First, there are too many people who need to know. Second, and most important, the people who need to know, rarely want to know. Which means that they just aren't ready to know. People who aren't ready for new information will reject it and may even belittle you for sharing it. Then resentment comes into play and everyone's good is slowed down. So be careful when you share your stuff. Don't force it on people. Let them come to you. People who really want to learn will automatically seek you out. When they do, willingly and loving share what you know.

However ...

Once you have agreed to teach someone or to become their mentor, you have a responsibility. You have a responsibility to be like the list that I just gave you, *and* you have the responsibility to stop any time someone doesn't follow what you say. It happens all the time. People want a mentor and then want to go it alone because they suddenly know better than the mentor. They will start to reject your ideas and argue with you. When that happens, let them go. Truth needs no defending. It doesn't have to be justified in any way. So when your mentee knows better or stops taking the advice that they asked for, lovingly release them. Again, *lovingly* release them.

CHAPTER

13

Love.

You cannot attract prosperity to yourself if you are filled with rancor, judgement, anger, jealously, hatred, fear, tension or the like. You cannot be fulfilled and envious at the same time.

Dr. Wayne Dyer

Follow the path of love, and all things are added, for God is love, and God is supply; follow the path of selfishness and greed, and the supply vanishes, or man is separated from it.

Florence Scovel Shinn

All you need is love. Love is all you need.

The Beatles

Goodness is the only investment that never fails.

Thoreau

Love is, above all, the gift of oneself.

Jean Anouilh

It is our willingness to be loving to ourselves and others that opens us to the true abundance of the Universe.

Arnold Patent

People don't come into your place of business so that you can get anything. They're sent so that you can give them love.

Marianne Williamson

Nothing will so quickly enrich your mind and free it from every thought of lack as the realization of divine love.

Charles Fillmore

Money comes from love. Money is made where love is present. When people join together in love and excitement and they are going to serve the planet together - that is where money comes from.

Marianne Williamson

> Love is the ultimate spiritual experience.
> Love is the greatest of all gifts.
> Love is the key to prosperity.

Some people are not lovable.

You got that right! My mother always said something that I really never completely understood until recently. She said, "You love people in spite of who they are and what they do, not because of who they are and what they do." Aren't mothers smart?

Let me give you something that helps me. Scope up. Get above the details of what people do. Look at them in a bigger way. Get a new perspective. Don't just see them as waiters, or salespeople, or flight attendants, or clerks, or drivers who have been rude to you. See them as people who are brothers and sisters, sons and daughters, husbands and wives, and mothers and fathers. Then see them as good people who are just having a bad day. Everyone has a bad day. Haven't you had a bad day that resulted in you being not very lovable?

We don't know the circumstances of others that cause them to act the way they do. Scope up. Think bigger than the moment. There is always more to it than you are able to see. People need our love much more than they need our judgemental criticism.

But why do they act that way?

People operate from either ignorance or knowledge. Jesus said, "Forgive them for they do not know what they do." (Luke 23:34) *and they don't!*

When people do things that you feel are inappropriate or harmful, they are operating from ignorance. People who offend you, take advantage of you, or hurt you in any way do so because they are operating from a limited knowledge and a limited awareness. They don't know any better. Even when they purposefully hurt others they are still operating from a lack of knowledge.

You don't get angry with babies when they burp in public do you? Of course not. But why not, isn't that inappropriate behavior? Not for babies, because they don't know any better. Other people don't know any better when they do something inappropriate either. They are just like the baby who doesn't understand. It is their nature to do those things because they are either ignorant of a better way, or they don't understand that their actions have consequences.

I know this isn't easy. Loving people when they do what we consider to be wrong is very hard. But unconditional love is the only answer to true happiness, success, prosperity and peace of mind.

More than lip service.

Love, as a word, is over used. We say that we love our car, our stereo, our clothes, and chocolate. It's not enough to say that you love this or that. We already do that way too much. When it comes to real Love, we have to do more than say it, we have to show it.

The issue in relationships is not just how much you love people, but how much they can feel your love.

Barbara De Angelis

How can I show love?

Accept people the way they are.

Simply say to yourself, "I expect nothing, because I know they can only be who they are, not what I think they should be," and proceed to act accordingly.

Dr. Wayne Dyer

People are what they are. Accept them. They aren't going to do things just the way you would do them. They aren't going to do things the way you want them to. They are just going to be themselves.

Everybody is who they are because that is who they are supposed to be at that moment. They must be who they are now so they can become who they ultimately must be later. In other words, we must all experience in life exactly what we are experiencing so we can grow and develop into the perfect person that we really are.

You had to go through all of the things you went through in the past in order to become who you are right now. Those experiences, good or bad, made you who you are right now. Treasure them. Bless them. Be thankful for them. Besides, you can't change any of them anyway.

So accept that same principle in others. Celebrate their uniqueness. Be glad that they are who they are. Because you know, even when they don't, that they are growing into the person they have the potential for being.

> Love others as you would be loved,
> treasuring them as they are,
> without expectations of change.
>
> Dick Sutphen

Forgive.

Forgiveness is the key to action and freedom.

Hannah Arendt

A forgiving attitude, with its ability to open hearts, is one of the most loving gifts we can ever give to ourselves.

Arnold Patent

Is it hard for you to forgive people? It always has been for me. In the past, when someone did something to me, I was always quick to let them know what they had done to me and then I usually went about getting even. Then I told everyone else about the dastardly deed and re-lived the experience several times so I could hold onto my misery to enjoy at a later date. Sound familiar to you? What a waste of time! Then I discovered that people are operating from ignorance and limited awareness. This helped me immensely. Then I realized another great truth.

When you get even with people by telling them off and giving them a piece of your mind, what you have really done is give them your *peace of mind.* Don't do that; they don't deserve it. Your peace of mind is worth way too much to you to waste it by getting mad or getting even. Love, forgive, and move on.

> Forgiveness in love is an absolute necessity for the successful demonstration of prosperity.
>
> Dr. James Melton

It's not personal.

People are rarely out to get you personally. You just aren't that important to them. They are just being the way they are, and you got in the way. Understanding this will make it much easier for you to forgive.

Unforgiveness will slow you down.

If you inflict your past wounds on the present, you'll make your future bleed.

Tom Hopkins

Unforgiveness is like a heavy weight that you have chosen to carry around. It keeps you from loving others fully and from loving yourself. It keeps you from being free to do and be your best. Unforgiveness will slow down your riches.

Make an "I Forgive" list.

Get a sheet of paper and start writing down the names of everyone in your life you need to forgive. Go back as far as you have to in order to get everybody. If a name even comes up that you have a question about, write it down. The list may contain your parents, family members, co-workers, business partners, ex-wives and ex-husbands, as well as current spouses and children. Some of the people on your list may be far removed. You may not have seen them or had any contact in years. Some may even be dead. That's okay. If you need to forgive them then write their name on your list.

Then sit quietly with the list and go through the list one by one and concentrate on completely forgiving this person. Let them go. Release the power that they hold over you. This is not an immediate process. It may be quick with some of the names on your list, but some will take time. Take all of the time you need. However, don't use the time to relive the hurt. Spend all of your time forgiving the hurt. Realize that people who hurt others are working from a position of ignorance and that people rarely set out to hurt you as an individual.

This is a personal process. It is not something that must ever involve the other person. The forgiveness must take place first in your heart and mind. Then if you need to outwardly forgive someone (you'll know) then do it. If it's too hard to say in person, then do it in writing. If you can't do that, then just keep it to yourself. But forgive.

Forgive Yourself.

Be sure that your "I Forgive" list includes your own name. Most of us live with the guilt of past mistakes. Guilt serves no purpose. You can't go back and change anything that was done. You can't fix it now. So forgive yourself. Stop carrying around the baggage of past mistakes and set yourself free.

There is no future in saying, "I should have" or "I could have" or "I wish I had" or "If only." You can't have a great future or even a great present when you are living in the mistakes of the past.

Change your "if only's" into "move ahead boldly's."

Dr. Robert Schuller

The mirror effect.

When you see something in someone else that needs to be forgiven, understand that they are only reflecting back to you what you need to forgive in yourself. They are acting as a mirror. If you see that you need to forgive someone for their impatience, it is an indicator that you have impatience in your life that needs to be forgiven. If you have been dealt with unfairly in a business deal, then look closely at the way you are conducting your own business dealings to see where you may need to work on yourself. You actually owe those who need to be forgiven a debt of gratitude for revealing to you what needs to be forgiven in yourself.

Or how can you say to your brother, "Let me remove the speck out of your eye;" and look, a plank is in your own eye?

Matthew 7: 4

Forgiving yourself is the place you have to start. So put your name
at the top of the list.

> ## You will forgive others to the same extent that you forgive yourself.

Turn the other cheek.

Jesus said to turn the other cheek. I always had a problem with that
one. I thought that it was self abuse and didn't reflect well on your
self image to willingly let someone beat up on you. Besides that, it's
painful! Then Marianne Williamson gave me a new interpretation
that said what it really meant was to look at the situation one way,
from your perspective, and then turn the other cheek and look at it
from the other person's perspective. There are always two ways to
see something. Try looking at things in a different way. A bigger
way. Start looking with new eyes; eyes of acceptance, understanding, forgiveness, and love.

Give up your need to be right.

*This is the single greatest cause of difficulties and deterioration in
relationships - the need to make the other person wrong, or to make
yourself right.*

Dr. Wayne Dyer

I enjoy being right.   In fact, I will go to almost any length to make
sure that I am right. I have always told myself that it was "the
principle of the thing." But as I became more enlightened in the
principles I am sharing with you in this book, I found that being
right just wasn't giving me the satisfaction that it once did. When
I realized that it was no longer necessary for me to prove myself
right, it was like a major weight had been lifted from my shoulders.

You don't build yourself up by tearing others down. There are no superiors or inferiors in life. We are all created as equals. We are all just doing our best with our limited knowledge. Our goal must be to love others and lift them up. We must never give in to the temptation to put another down. In doing so we tear ourselves down even more.

Do you prefer to be right or happy?

A Course In Miracles

Encouragement.

To encourage someone means "to put courage into them." It is hard for me to imagine any better way to show love than to help someone have the courage to be more, do more, and have more. Encourage others through your smile, your friendship, your words, and your help.

Respect.

Respect is another form of love. Respect for the opinions of other people. Respect for their ideas and what they have to say. This doesn't mean that you have to agree or disagree with them. It just says that you should have respect for who they are and what they represent.

Respect is for everyone, not just friends, business associates, and special groups of people. It is for the transient on the street corner, the rude person at the grocery store, and the obnoxious customer. One of the most forgotten areas of respect is in the family. So respect your spouse and your children. Respect their ideas, their good days and bad days, their privacy, and their need to express their individualism.

Listen.

One of the greatest gifts you can give anyone is to listen to them.
Listen without judging what they are saying in any way. Listen
without agreement or disagreement. Just listen to them with
genuine interest, even when you think that what they are saying is
probably the dumbest thing you have ever heard come out of
anyone's mouth. Listen as though this was the most interesting
thing you have ever heard. Love the person and pay little mind to
what they are saying if you must, but show them that you are at least
listening and watch how warmly they will respond. People love to
have their opinions noted. They love to know that they are being
listened to. You can do that for them. A relatively small thing for
you and a real act of love for them.

Be excellent at what you do.

Doing what you do to the best of your ability is an act of love. It
shows that you are serious about giving your employer your best
and that you love your employer. Being excellent at what you do
also shows that you are committed to being your best and providing
the best product and service for your customer. That is an act of
love. It also shows that you love yourself enough to do the best you
can with the abilities you have.

"Thou shalt not steal."

When you do less than your best, you are stealing. You are stealing
from your employer, your customer, and yourself.

When you do less than your best then you haven't really performed
in a manner that justifies your earning all that you are being paid.
That is stealing.

When you haven't done your best then you have produced a product or provided a service that is less than the customer is paying for and expecting. That too is stealing.

When you have done less than your best, you have cheated yourself of the pleasure you will receive from knowing that you have done your best. You have stolen from yourself.

In each case, you have not acted from a spirit of love.

Your real business.

You may think that you are in the insurance business, or the telecommunications business, or the food business. You may believe that your business is selling copiers, or being a dentist, or being a professional speaker. You are wrong. Those things are only what you do as you carry out your real business.

Your real business is the business of loving and serving. Focus on this and success is guaranteed. Love others and you will sell more insurance, telephone systems, or copiers than you ever thought possible. Understand that love is the best selling principle that exists. Love will win you achievement awards. Love will make you the Employee of the Year. Love will make you rich. Love is your real business.

The four loves.

Love what you do.

Love what you do or do something that you love. You will never be excellent at doing something that you don't enjoy doing.

Love the people you do it for.

This includes your company or employer as well as your customer. You have to love both of these if you are ever going to be truly successful and prosperous.

Love the product or service you provide.

Love the end result of the work you love to do. Know that what you provide serves others well.

Love yourself.

When you love yourself you will treat yourself well physically, mentally and spiritually. You will expect the best from yourself and do your best at all times.

> Let the river of your life flow freely and deeply, and let the pebbles of your love fall into the water to create ripples that will touch us all.
>
> Bernie Siegel, M.D.

CHAPTER

14

Serve.

I don't know what your destiny will be, but one thing I do know; the only ones among you who will be truly happy will be those who have sought and found how to serve.

Albert Schweitzer

Consciously or unconsciously, every one of us does render some service or other. If we cultivate the habit of doing this service deliberately, our desire for service will steadily grow stronger, and will make not only for our own happiness, but that of the world at large.

Gandhi

God can only do for you what He can do through you.

Eric Butterworth

Success means we go to sleep at night knowing that our talents and abilities were used in a way that served others.

Marianne Williamson

In being of spiritual, mental, and material service to others, you will find your own needs fulfilled. As you forget self in service to others, you will find that, without seeking it, your own cup of happiness will be full.

Paramahansa Yogananda

Unless life is lived for others, it is not worthwhile.

Mother Teresa

The measure of a man is in the number of people whom he serves.

Paul D. Moody

We are here to serve one another by giving generously of our talents and rendering services or creating products that express these talents. The natural result of this process is that money and other material wealth flows into our lives.

Arnold Patent

The problem with the word.

One of the ways that the dictionary defines the word "serve" is "to be a servant." Most people have a problem with that. We don't usually like to think of ourselves as servants. It carries a demeaning connotation that tends to have us think of ourselves as lower than another person. Discard this thinking now.

Serving others is the most honorable act you can perform. It is anything but demeaning. It is an act based in Love.

Who do you serve?

More than 99% of all the men and women who have achieved wealth have done it by utilizing their talents and abilities to the maximum in the service of other people.

Brian Tracy

Customer service is one of the hottest business topics around. Therefore, we tend to think of the word service from a purely business standpoint: customer service. However, serving must go beyond business and that is where it gets a little more complicated.

You serve your employer. You are paid for the service you provide your employer. The level of service you provide will determine your income, position, and advancement.

You serve your co-workers. When you do your job effectively you have created a high quality product that will then become the product for another person or department. Your outgoing product, no matter what it might be, becomes the incoming product for someone else. Someone else's outgoing product has become your incoming product. We are all interconnecting links and form a giant chain that results in a final product that is then sold to a customer.

You serve your family. You provide for them. You offer them love, support, and friendship as well as all of the tangibles like food, clothing and housing.

You serve other people. You serve the people with whom you have close relationships like your friends as well as those you come in contact with on a more casual basis. You also serve those faceless people you come in contact with every day by the hundreds. Your every action serves in some way.

You serve the Universe. The work you provide, the people you influence, your thoughts, words, and deeds all impact the Universe in some way.

You serve yourself. You take care of yourself mentally, spiritually and physically. The degree to which you do this will determine how well you are able to function in the world.

There are many ways to serve.

The number of opportunities to relieve suffering is as great as the number of sufferings themselves.

Ram Dass

To put this another way, there are as many ways to solve problems as there are problems. So don't complicate this idea of serving. When you live a life of service, everything you do is a service.

A smile is a service you render. Who wouldn't enjoy a smile? A hug for a friend in need is a service. A friendly look and a word of encouragement are both ways of serving others.

> Your rewards in life are
> in direct proportion
> to your service.
> Earl Nightingale

Serving is solving problems.

Problems are wonderful opportunities to serve. Problems are the key to your significance. In fact, problems will determine the amount of money you make in life.

If a person makes five dollars an hour, then they are probably solving five dollar problems and it takes them about an hour to do it.

If a person makes five thousand dollars an hour, then they are probably solving five thousand dollar problems and it takes them about an hour to do it.

If you want to make more money, increase the size of the problem you solve. Or learn to solve more problems of the same size in a shorter period of time. In other words, add more value. When the value is increased the reward will be increased.

Money is the symbol of duty, it is the sacrament of having done for mankind that which mankind wanted.

Samuel Butler

Service is a form of Love.

When you serve, you have loved. When you love, you have served. Look closely at the chapter on Love. Review the various ways that I suggest you show love. The same principles apply to serving.

Love All. Serve All.

Sign above the kitchen
Hard Rock Cafe
Washington, D.C.

CHAPTER

15

Give.

The moment that you realize that giving is the key to your own abundance, you will also see that prosperity is readily available.

Dr. Wayne Dyer

In tithing we sow seeds of prosperity, and the harvest is certain.

L. E. Meyer

Earn all you can, save all you, give all you can.

John Wesley

Where there is giving and sharing with no fear of lack, there is always plenty.

Winifred Hausmann

Give freely, joyously, lovingly, and with a sense of abandonment, and as you do, fabulous wealth inevitably will be yours.

Joseph Murphy

You can double your living by doubling your giving.

Sig Paulson

Most of us think that when we give it will diminish and deplete our resources, leaving us with less than we had. But I have learned that it is only what you give that will increase . . . only what you give can God multiply, and when He does, He does it abundantly!

Oral Roberts

When God speaks through your hands and smiles upon the earth through you, because you are an unconditional giver, a purposeful being, asking nothing of anyone, prosperity will be your reward.

Dr. Wayne Dyer

Nature abhors a vacuum.

In order to have more of the good stuff in your life you must make room for it. That means that you have to give some of the stuff that you currently have away. When you give your stuff away you have created a vacuum and Nature will spring into action to fill that vacuum.

This Universal Law will work with anything that you have or need. So look closely at what you have. Regardless of how meager the quantity may seem to be, start to give some of it away and watch how it will be replaced in bigger quantities. Don't bother trying to refute this principle. It is a Law. Therefore, it will work every time.

Give money.

Let me share with you an incredible demonstration of the power of giving in my own life. (This story has been previously released in my book, *The Simple Way To Success.*)

After my business failure, I was broke. So broke I couldn't even pay attention. Because of that, I immediately got out of the habit of giving. Probably a response that most people could easily justify. However, as justifiable as it may have been, it still wasn't right. This "no giving" attitude/excuse I had developed became a new habit with me and continued even after I started experiencing success in my speaking career.

While one of the principles I was speaking on was The Law of Reciprocity, I just couldn't seem to bring myself to give up any of my money. It had taken too long to start having any money again and I just found it impossible to give away any of what I had accumulated.

One day as I sat in my office, I had an absolutely overwhelming urge to break this habit and give some money to my church. The amount I felt to compelled to give was one hundred dollars. While that isn't a lot of money, at the time it seemed a huge amount, especially since it was one hundred dollars more than I had given in a very long while. Plus, it seemed that I just had so many bills and other obligations and Christmas was coming and I needed to spend my money on so many others things. (Probably excuses that you have used before too, right?) Well, I followed my "feeling" and immediately wrote out the check for one hundred dollars, stuck it in an envelope, addressed it, and put a stamp on it. I became so afraid that I was going to back out on sending it that I got in my car and took it immediately to the Post Office. I felt great about doing it. I just knew that it was the right thing for me to do.

That night at my home, my doorbell rang. It was my attorney. Since most attorneys don't make house calls, I wondered what in the world he wanted. I invited him in and he told me that day he had a large debt forgiven him, and he wanted to pass on his good fortune by forgiving one of his debtors. So he had stopped by my house to tell me personally that he was forgiving the balance on my account. The balance on my account was **one hundred dollars!**

I know many people would say that I had just experienced an interesting coincidence. However, I will never be convinced of that. I know that I had just experienced The Law first hand. That event forever changed my attitude toward giving.

You can't afford not to be generous and giving of your time, efforts, talents, and money. Prosperity flows. Open up the channels!

Another slant on giving.

Give whatever you lack. If you lack money, give money. If you lack time, give time. If you lack love, give love. Give away business. Sound silly? You may be saying, "If I had enough of it to give away

then I would happily give it." I contend that if you would happily
give it, then you would have more than enough of it to give away.
I find that the more business I give away, the more business I have.
I have found that the best way for me to receive love is to give love
first. This principle will work in any area of your personal or
professional life. Remember the vacuum. Create space for more in
your life by giving what you have away.

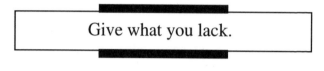

Give what you lack.

Give yourself.

*You give but little when you give possessions, it is when you give of
yourself that you truly give.*

Kahlil Gibran

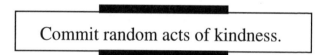

Commit random acts of kindness.

Lovingly give yourself away. Give yourself to your job, your
customers, your family, your spouse, your friends, to strangers and
to the world.

Motive.

Many prosperity teachers talk about giving with the right motive.
Some say that if you give out of a sense of obligation, or duty, or if
you give in order to get, then you are wasting your time. Some even
say that if you give because you really enjoy it, that you aren't really
giving at all but are just buying the enjoyment.

I disagree. I think that you should give willingly, cheerfully, and with a spirit of love. However, I think that the very act of giving, regardless of motive, is an act of love and will be rewarded.

I believe that the Law of Sowing and Reaping just says *give.* It's a Law. A Law that says if you don't sow you have no right to expect to reap. A Law that says to look at your harvest and then look at what you planted. If you didn't harvest much, you didn't plant much. So as Jim Rohn says, "You had better get some sowing going!"

Give, and it will be given to you; good measure, pressed down, shaken together, and running over will be put into your bosom. For with the same measure that you use, it will be measured back to you.
Luke 6:38

The only condition I have found to giving is that our attitude be right about it. We should give cheerfully.

Be a cheerful giver.

So let each one give as he purposes in his heart, not grudgingly or of necessity; for God loves a cheerful giver.

And the promise is:

And God is able to make all grace abound toward you, that you, always having sufficiency in all things, have an abundance for every good work.
2 Corinthians 9: 7,8

When we give with the right attitude we are given a promise that we will be provided for *in all things!*

> A rejected opportunity to give
> is a lost opportunity to receive.
>
> Oral Roberts

Become attractive.

Everything you have in your life is there because you attracted it.
Mike Wickett

You have what you have because you attracted it to you; your friends, your house, your car, your stuff, your money. It is all there as a reflection of your attractiveness.

> Money comes to those who have
> made themselves attractive to money.

How it works.

Like attracts like. You have probably heard different. You have probably heard that opposites attract. True. Opposites do attract, but not for long. The bottom line is that long term relationships are based on commonality. While differences are normal, intriguing and interesting, it's the stuff you share that is the bond for long term relationships. This includes your relationships with people and money. If you are constantly saying and doing things that repel prosperity, then don't be surprised that you are broke. Remember, like attracts like. Success attracts success. Money - even a very small amount, when spoken well of, loved and appreciated, given freely, and circulated with confidence - attracts more money.

The good, the bad, and the ugly.

When we have something really good happen to us that we have been involved in, it is very easy for us to take credit for the good thing. We love to say how we made it happen - how because of us this good thing came to be. We enjoy taking complete responsibility for the achievement.

Are we as quick to take responsibility for the stuff that doesn't turn out so good? I doubt it. It is so easy to lay blame elsewhere. However, we must understand that our experiences, whether good, bad, or ugly, have happened because we attracted them to ourselves though our state of consciousness, our thoughts, beliefs, words, appearance, and actions.

So what do I do?

In order to attract anything, you must first become attractive. Make yourself attractive to good things. People like to do business with and be around and help winners - look like a winner.

Appearance.

People on the corner with "Will Work For Food" signs are making a mistake. Most have a sincere need in their lives to have more. However, they are operating from a level of poverty thinking and misunderstanding. They don't seem to understand that their very appearance, which is a result of their thinking, keeps them from having enough. If they would clean up and become more attractive they would increase their chances of getting hired and could then work for money. Then they could buy food and the other things that they want and deserve. My heart goes out to these people. They need our love, support, and encouragement. They need a change of thinking. They need to think of themselves as worthwhile deserving people. This will then reflect itself in how they look and will increase their attractiveness to the world and to prosperity.

I see this same problem every day in people from all walks of life. People who don't think well of themselves reflect it through their uncleanliness. Salespeople who call on you with a terrific product, yet have dirty fingernails, aren't making themselves attractive to your business. Those people just won't do as well as they could.

Does this stuff really matter? You bet it does. You must become attractive physically in order to attract the best. That means you have to clean up. Smell good. Brush your teeth. Take care of your breath. Shine your shoes. Lose some weight if you need to.

This also means that you should dress as well as you possibly can. You don't have to spend a fortune to look good and to be in style. There is fashionable clothing in every price range. Get some help if you don't know what is in style. People judge you visually first. How you look is important. They won't take the time to find out what's on the inside of you if the outside of you repels them.

When I was in the telecommunications business, I put an ad in the newspaper for a telephone installer. This was at a time when there was an overabundance of people available in the field to pick from so I was overwhelmed with applicants. As I began the task of interviewing these people, it became evident without a word being said who was really interested in getting the job. There were those who showed up for the interview wearing dirty jeans. While these people were sometimes the best qualified from a technical stand-point, I would always ask myself the question, "If this is the way they look when they ask for the job, how will they look when they get the job?" I was also concerned what my customers would think about my company, me, and the systems we were installing for them, based on the appearance of this individual as their installer.

That's when I called into my office a person who truly stood out from the rest. He wore a suit. Not a great suit or an expensive suit, but a suit. He walked in with enthusiasm and looked me in the eye and gave me a great big smile. Under his arm he carried a box. When he opened the box, it was full of certificates of past training, letters from employers, and testimonials from satisfied customers. No one else had brought anything like that. However, the most interesting thing of all was not that he brought these pieces of paper in, but that each one was in a frame. He had taken these off of his wall in his home and brought them in for me to see because he was proud of them.

He over-dressed for the interview. While it would never again be necessary for him to wear a suit on the job, he wanted to make himself as attractive as possible. He also showed pride in who he was by bringing with him framed documentation of his past accomplishments. Who got the job? He did, of course. He made himself attractive and the job was attracted to him.

It's your face, too.

There is more to making your appearance attractive than clothes. There is your face. This includes your eye contact and your smile. Look people in the eye when you talk to them. It shows that you have confidence in yourself and what you are talking about. It will increase the perception that you are a person who can be trusted.

Smile. Smile whether you feel like it or not. People like doing business with people who are friendly. A smile makes you feel better and it will make the other person feel better. It will disarm tense situations better than almost any other tool. Your eye contact and your smile will make you more attractive.

Attitude.

Are you automatically attracted to negative, discouraging people? I doubt it. I have yet to see someone intentionally go into a room and look for the most negative person there to hang around with. Most people are more drawn to people who are positive.

Do you find negative people drawn to you? They are drawn to you because that is the kind of person you are. Understand that they are only reflecting back to you what you are showing them. If you want positive people to surround you, then become positive and those kind of people will start to flock around you.

In an earlier chapter, I discussed attitudes toward money. People that are of like attitudes about money will be attracted to you. Look at your circle of friends. I'll bet that they are all of a very similar belief system and have many of the same attitudes about life and money that you do. If this is true, and you don't like what you have, then you might consider getting a new group of friends. You do that by changing your attitude. Your old friends will automatically drift away because you are no longer like them and new friends with similar attitudes will appear in your life.

Make your spoken word attractive.

We should make ourselves attractive by wearing the fine garment of genuinely courteous language.

Paramahansa Yogananda

Your attitude will also be reflected in how you speak to others. Learn to say please and thank you. Be courteous to everyone you meet. Speak well of others. In order to build a successful business we must:

Create an environment where we only speak well of others, ourselves, and the customer.

We should carry this beyond the workplace into the world and remember to only speak well of ourselves and other people in all situations. This means that we shouldn't become involved in gossip or speak unkindly of anyone else at any time. Only speak of others in a manner that you would want them to speak of you.

Be on a mission.

Did you ever see someone who just drew people to them like a magnet? What is that magnet? I believe that the magnet is purpose. Purpose means that you are on a mission. It is a love for what you do, a love for the people you do it for, and a belief and confidence in your ability to do it. That's attractive. It will attract customers, friends and money.

Tag yourself a winner.

A few years ago, I got a personalized license plate for my car. It said WINNER. I had no idea at the time, the impact that plate would have on my life. I found out that with a tag on your car that says WINNER, you can no longer do the things you have been used to doing. You can no longer pull out in traffic a little too fast and cut someone off (not that I would ever do that). Why not? Would a WINNER cut someone off in traffic? No, only a loser would do that. Would a WINNER honk at someone who was slow pulling away from a red light? No, only a loser would do that. Would a WINNER even drive a dirty car? No! I had tagged myself a WINNER for the whole world to see and suddenly my actions had to change to live up to that label. I became more winner-like all because I had proclaimed I was a winner.

What a lesson. Call yourself something and you will become more like that something. What do you call yourself? Do you call yourself a loser? Broke? Poor? Is your life full of can'ts, won'ts, should have's, would have's, I wish I had's, and if only's? Then that is the kind of life you will attract because you have proclaimed that to be true about yourself.

When you want to attract the life of a prosperous, happy person then proclaim that about yourself and it will happen. Tag yourself a winner and you will begin to act like a winner and will attract the life of a winner.

> We attract to us what we first become.

CHAPTER

17

The Law.

You can have everything in life you want if you will just help enough other people get what they want.

Zig Ziglar

Your rewards in life are in direct proportion to your service.

Earl Nightingale

For every action there is an equal and opposite reaction.

The Law of Cause and Effect

. . . for whatsoever a man sows, that he will also reap.

Galations 6:7

What goes around, comes around.

Almost everybody

This chapter could also be called How Life Works, but I already used that title. However, make no mistake about this Law, it *is* how life works! The Law rules the world. It rules your life. It is the reason you have what you have right now.

Every effect in your life has a cause. You are responsible for those causes. You determine your causes by controlling your thinking and your beliefs. The Law is the underlying principle that holds all of the principles I've covered in this book together. Success in serving, loving, giving, and forgiving are all based on The Law of Reciprocity. Life is reciprocal. See how it all ties together? What goes out from you in any form must inevitably come back to you.

Good news!

You can't break this Law. There is simply no way to break it. The Law says that you reap what you sow. Well, there is no way to not sow anything. You just can't do it. Even if you sit on the couch 24 hours a day and do nothing, you are sowing. You are sowing lots of nothingness. It's not hard to figure out what the reward for that kind of sowing will be.

You are always putting a cause into effect. Lousy cause - lousy effect. Magnificent cause - magnificent effect. There is no way to escape this. Therefore, there is no way to break this law. It is always working in every area of your life and at all times. Remember the statement I used earlier in the book, "Like it or not, you always get results."

The Law is neutral.

The Law of Cause and Effect, being no respecter of persons and always working automatically and mechanically and with mathematical precision, must flow through each one of us in terms of our own acceptance.

Ernest Holmes

The Law doesn't play favorites. It doesn't like me more than it likes you, nor does it like you more than it likes me. In fact, it doesn't like or dislike anyone. The Law just is. Period. You can make it work for you or you can cause it to work against you. It is your choice.

The Law doesn't know amounts.

The Law doesn't care whether you use it to demonstrate a million dollars or one dollar. The Law works the very same in both cases. The people who use it to get the million only understand it better, use it more, and believe in it more. That's the difference.

According to your faith let it be to you.

Matthew 9: 29

Sow a little, reap a little. Sow a lot, reap a lot.

He who sows sparingly will also reap sparingly; and he who sows bountifully will also reap bountifully.

2 Corinthians 9: 6

If you don't have enough you haven't sown enough. If you need more in your life give more. If you want to have more then do more.

Pretty simple idea isn't it? I told you in the introduction of this book that the principles for acquiring more were not complicated.

The Universe is an experience of ease and simplicity. One of the ways that you know you are dealing with universal principles is that the concepts are simple and easy.

Arnold Patent

Don't fight it.

Success is the most natural thing in the world. The person who does not succeed has placed himself in opposition to the Laws of the Universe.

Elbert Hubbard

It will do you no good to resist the Law. You don't have to like it, agree with it, or even be knowledgeable of it, the Law will always win. The Law governs everything in your life. Learn to work with it. Accept it. Embrace it. Use it.

Change it.

If you don't like who you are, change it. If you aren't happy with what you have, change it. If you don't like what you are doing, change it.

You know how. You know the Law. You have the Power! Begin to use the Law in every area of your life. Think about how the Law has already worked in your life to give you the experiences that you have. Play with it. Experiment with it. Test it. You'll see that it always works. Begin to rely on it and know that the use of the Law can change your life!

No, it won't be easy. Of course, you will slip and fall back into old habits and thinking patterns. Yes, you will have to focus and read and study and meditate. But the rewards will all be worth it!

Every choice has a consequence.
By taking note of the consequences,
we can decide to choose differently.

Arnold Patent

Study Prosperity.

In order to have more, do more. In order to do more, become more!
A Universal Principle

If you feed your mind as often as you feed your stomach, then you'll never have to worry about feeding your stomach or a roof over your head or clothes on your back.
Albert Einstein

True preparation for wealth is in the mind. Ideas are the coins of the mind realm. Make your mind the abiding place of rich thoughts.
Ernest E. Wilson

If you wanted to become a Doctor what would you study? Medicine, of course. If you wanted to become a lawyer, you would study the law. If you wanted to become a welder, you would study welding. And if you want to become prosperous, you should study prosperity!

Make a study of what you want to become. Focus on the principles of prosperity as discovered by someone else. Take advantage of the knowledge that has already been recorded. Gain from the experience of other people.

Show me what a person pays attention to and I'll tell you what their intentions are.
Joseph J. Charbonneau

What are you paying attention to? If your intentions are to be wealthy, then start paying attention to what it takes to become that way!

Money Is Easy Reading and Listening List.

Read the books and listen to the tapes that are suggested at the end of this book. I own each of the books listed and use them as constant resources. The tapes I have listed should be listened to over and over again in order to get the maximum benefit. In fact, if you will listen only six times to each of them, you will retain as much as ninety percent of the information.

Act immediately.

When you get a new piece of information, and you will get many as you read these books, put that information to use immediately. Don't wait to get a hundred good ideas before beginning. Don't wait for ten or even two. Every good idea should be implemented immediately. Sometimes it only takes one good idea to make a drastic difference in your life and your income.

No excuses.

"But I can't afford to buy all of those books and tapes." Stop whining, and quit saying "I can't afford it!" You can't afford *not* to buy these books and tapes! You don't have to buy them all at once. Start by just buying one. Read it, act on it, and then go get another one.

Buy them! Don't check them out at the library and don't borrow them. You need to demonstrate your belief in yourself and your pending wealth by *buying* the books. If you bought every book on the Money Is Easy Suggested Reading List you would have spent only about three hundred dollars. Three hundred dollars that could teach you the principles for having millions!

When you own the books you can mark in them and takes notes and scribble in the margins. You can participate actively in the book. So go buy the books. Buy the tapes. Demonstrate your commitment and belief that you are going to be rich.

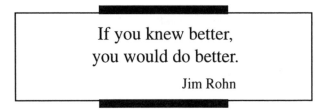

If you knew better,
you would do better.

Jim Rohn

It really can happen to you.

Whatever you want wants you.

Mark Victor Hansen

The great truth is that there is a Divine Plan for your life . . . it includes health, happiness, abundance, and perfect self-expression.

Catherine Ponder

It is your right to be rich. You are here to lead the abundant life and be happy, radiant, and free. You should, therefore, have all the money you need to lead a full, happy, and prosperous life.

Joseph Murphy

To hold one's thoughts steadfastly to the constructive, to that which endures, and to the Truth, may not be easy in a rapidly changing world, but to the one who makes the attempt much is guaranteed.

Ernest Holmes

Why not you?

If it can happen to anyone, it can happen to you. The Universe has no favorites. The abundance of the world is available for everybody. There is no reason for you not to have everything you want and need.

There is no excuse for you to have less than plenty and not more than enough.

Why it will work for you.

The ideas I have given you in this book are principles. Principles are timeless. They always work. Any time. Every time. Principles are universal. They will work for anyone. Principles are neutral. They don't play favorites and are completely available for anyone willing to use them. All you have to do is work the principle and the principle will work for you. In fact, there is no way that the principles won't work . Accept this as fact. Don't just believe it, know it. Know that it's true for you!

The key to making it happen.

Two words will make it happen for you. Suspend disbelief. If belief can make it happen, and it can, it stands to reason that disbelief can keep it from happening. So let go of disbelief. It hasn't made you any money yet so why are you holding on to it?

Suspend Disbelief.

How much is enough?

No amount is ever enough. You can't measure your financial success or any other area of success in amounts. The only way to know how much is enough is when you have done your best. Only your best is enough.

Is $150,000 per year enough? Not if your full potential would be to make $150, 000, 000 per year. If your best is in the millions and you make in the thousands, then you are not living up to your best and fullest potential. By not giving yourself and others the best you are cheating everyone concerned.

Is $10,000 enough? It's plenty if you received it as a result of giving your very best.

Have you served your best? Did you love as much as you possibly could? Did you give your best? When you have believed the best, done your best, given, loved and served your best, then what you have received is enough.

Get this part.

Everything either moves you closer to where you want to be or farther away from where you want to be. Everything. Every action, conversation, relationship, every word, and every thought. Every belief you have moves you closer to your prosperity or farther away from your prosperity. *Nothing is neutral.*

Every thought you have contributes to truth or to illusion; either it extends the truth or it multiplies the illusions.

A Course In Miracles

Closely examine your actions and your thoughts. Understand that everything moves you closer to your prosperity or farther away from your prosperity. Let go of everything that moves you farther away. Suspend your disbelief and begin now to claim the riches and abundance that are yours.

Declare to yourself often:

Every day in every way I am growing more prosperous, successful, victorious. I am made for peace, health, and plenty, and I am now experiencing them in ever-increasing degrees in my life!

Catherine Ponder

In summary.

You may have figured out by now that this book is not primarily about money; this book is about you. The amount of money you have will change when you change. Money is just a by-product of your thoughts, beliefs, words, and actions. Money is a natural occurrence in the life of someone who lives purposefully in a spirit of love, service, and giving.

Not

The End.

The

Beginning.

More Money Is Easy

For God's gift to you, is more talent and ability, than you will ever use in one lifetime. Your gift to God is to develop and utilize as much of that talent and ability as you can, in this lifetime.

Bob Proctor

If you want prosperity, then claim everyday that God is your prosperity and the Giver of every good gift, that God knows you and is ready to more than supply your every need.

Emmet Fox

Anything that will enable us to express greater life, greater happiness, greater power - so long as it does not harm anyone - must be the Will of God for us. As much life as one can conceive will become a part of his experience.

Ernest Holmes

Life is for you and me. It is ready to give us whatever we claim; whatever we aim for we will obtain.

Mark Victor Hansen

With love and enthusiasm directed toward our work, what was once a chore and hardship now becomes a wonderful tool to develop, enrich, and nourish our lives.

Jerry Gillies

It is useless to affirm benefits, protection, supply, guidance, and healing, if all the time you are doing things which you know are not right in the sight of God and man.

Catherine Ponder

Nothing but your own thoughts can hamper your progress.

A Course In Miracles

If we believe, absolutely, that we can do a certain thing, the way will be opened for us to do it. If we believe that time has to elapse before we can achieve it, then we are making that a law, and time will have to elapse. If, on the other hand, we believe that Divine Mind knows just how to do it and never makes mistakes, and we accept this action, then it will be done now.

Ernest Holmes

What we think determines what we believe; what we believe influences what we choose; what we choose defines what we are; and what we are attracts what we have.

Jim Rohn

Most people think they want more money than they really do, and settle for a lot less than they could get.

Earl Nightingale

If you ask for success and prepare for failure, you will receive the thing you have prepared for.

Florence Scovel Shinn

Thoughts of lack manifest as limitation. Thoughts of abundance manifest as success and happiness.

Ernest Holmes

Any idea that is held in the mind that is either feared or revered will begin at once to clothe itself in the most convenient and appropriate physical forms available.

Andrew Carnegie

Whatever you expect to happen is determined by the thoughts and the emotions behind those thoughts.

Dr. Robert Anthony

Lack and limitation can only exist when we make room for them in our minds. But prosperity consciousness knows no lack and limitation.

Bob Proctor

Those who practice tithing will have more to give than they thought possible before. Tithing shows a willingness to work with the law of prosperity and to return to the giver at least a part of that which He has given to us.

L. E. Meyer

The connection between tithing and prosperity is, after all, but a particular expression of the general law that what we are to the universe, that will the universe be to us; that what we give out, whether it be generosity or parsimony, that we shall receive back; that like attracts like; that whatsoever a man soweth, that shall he also reap; and that no man escapes the Law.

Emmet Fox

Any fact facing us is not as important as our attitude toward it, for that determines our success or failure.

Dr. Norman Peale

It's not your aptitude but your attitude that determines you altitude.

Jesse Jackson

Prosperity is not the result of following a strict set of gimmicks and strategies, it is a mind-set that is centered on your ability to manifest miracles.

Dr. Wayne Dyer

Life is not made up of the have's and the have-not's - but of the will's and the will-not's.

Larry Winget

You give not as a debt you owe, but as a seed you sow!

Oral Roberts

You create opportunities for yourself. The greatest tragedy in your life is to think you have no choices. Your future choices expand as you choose to be more, do more and live more.

Mark Victor Hansen

The best thing you can do
for the poor is to not be one of them.

Reverend Ike

Mental awareness of prosperity always precedes wealth in your material world.

Bob Proctor

When you believe something you have made it true for you.

A Course In Miracles

For if we think poverty and lack we are certainly creating them and causing them to be projected into our experience. If, on the other hand, we think abundance, then the Law will as easily and as willingly create abundance for us.

Ernest Holmes

When we get frightened, we want to control everything, and then we shut off the flow of our good. Trust life. Everything we need is here for us.

Louise Hay

If I dwell on limitation and insufficiency in any area of my life, I am building a consciousness of lack, and lack always attracts more lack.

John Randolph Price

Money - like health, love, happiness and all forms of miraculous happenings that you want to create for yourself - is the result of living purposefully.

Dr. Wayne Dyer

Real prosperity is more than money. It is a state of mind and a standard of living. To achieve total prosperity you will want to be financially, mentally, physically, emotionally, socially and spiritually well-off.

Mark Victor Hansen

For when you succeed in convincing your subconscious mind that you are wealthy and that it feels good to be wealthy, your subconscious mind will automatically seek ways of making your "imaginary" feelings of wealth manifest themselves in material form.

Bob Proctor

You continually look for ways to give your love, your talent, your time, and earnings - anything that represents you. You give until it becomes a part of you . . . giving in joy . . . without grudging. And God multiplies the seed sown - the gift given - back to you in the form of your personal needs.

Oral Roberts

The secret of demonstrating prosperity in the spiritual way - and on no other basis can your prosperity ever be secure - is to understand, that is, to know to the point of realization, that the one and only source of your supply is God, and that your business or employment, your investments, your clients or customers, are but the particular channel through which that supply is at the moment coming to you from God.

Emmet Fox

There is no happiness in having or getting, but only in giving.

Henry Drummond

Money is God in action.

Reverend Ike

Most of the things money is the root of ain't evil.

Malcolm Forbes

A person acting from a motivation
of contribution and service rises to
such a level or moral authority,
that worldly success is a natural result.

Marianne Williamson

The abundant life for each individual is the Will of God. God is the source of all prosperity and is forever providing us with whatever we need in abundant measure.

John Randolph Price

Curse the rich and you won't be one of us.

Reverend Ike

Money is a very excellent servant, but a terrible master.

P. T. Barnum

There is nothing more demoralizing than a small but adequate income.

Edmund Wilson

I believe that the power to make money is a gift from God.
                                             John D. Rockefeller

Mastering nonattachment requires the willingness to believe that the Universe is a place of abundance. Until we arrive at that belief, we create circumstances that validate what we do believe. When we finally recognize that abundance is our natural state of being, we release all attachments to our mental abundance and then it flows freely into our lives.
                                             Arnold Patent

Man is only truly great when he acts from passion.
                                             B. Disraeli

Thoughts of lack, poverty and limitation contain within themselves the conditions necessary to produce lack, poverty and limitation.
                                             Ernest Holmes

First comes thought, then organization of that thought into ideas and plans; then transformation of those plans into reality. The beginning, as you will observe, is in your imagination.
                                             Napoleon Hill

Keep away from people who try to belittle your ambitions. Small people always do that, but the really great make you feel that you, too, can become great.
                                             Mark Twain

Keep on succeeding, for only successful people can help others.
                                             Robert Schuller

Sow a thought, reap an action; sow an action, reap a habit; sow a habit, reap a character; sow a character reap a destiny.
                                             Ralph Waldo Emerson

The lack of money is the root of all evil.
                                             George Bernard Shaw

What's wrong with money? Having none.

Malcolm Forbes

All of the money you are ever going to have is currently in the hands of someone else.

Earl Nightingale

The word gives form to the unformed. The greater the consciousness behind the word, the more power it will have.

Ernest Holmes

We find our happiness not in solving all the problems of the world, but in ceasing to be one of those problems.

J. Kennedy Shultz

Live long and prosper.
The Vulcan Creed, Star Trek

Money Is Easy Reading List

The Bible.

Anthony, Robert Dr. **Dr. Robert Anthony's Advanced Formula For Total Success.** New York, New York: Berkley Books, 1973.

Butterworth, Eric. **Spiritual Economics.** Unity Village, Missouri: Unity School of Christianity, 1983.

Chopra, Deepak. **Creating Affluence.** San Rafael, California: New World Library, 1993.

Clason, George S. **The Richest Man In Babylon.** New York: Hawthorn Books, 1955.

Dyer, Wayne. **Real Magic.** New York, New York: HarperCollins Publishers, Inc. 1992.

Dyer, Wayne. **You'll See It When You Believe It.** New York, New York: Avon Books, 1989.

Fillmore, Charles. **Prosperity.** Unity Village, Missouri: Unity Books, 1936.

Fisher, Mark. **The Instant Millionaire.** San Rafael, California: New World Library, 1990.

Fox, Emmet. **Stake Your Claim.** New York, New York: Harper & Row, 1952.

Gillies, Jerry. **Moneylove.** New York, New York: Warner Books, 1978.

Hansen, Mark Victor. **How To Achieve Total Prosperity.** Newport Beach, California: Mark Victor Hansen and Associates, 1981.

Hill, Napoleon. **Think And Grow Rich.** North Hollywood, California: Wilshire Book Company, 1966.

Holmes, Ernest. **The Science Of Mind.** New York, New York: G. P. Putnam's Sons, 1938.

John-Roger and Peter McWilliams. **Wealth 101.** Los Angeles, California: Prelude Press, 1992.

Laut, Phil. **Money Is My Friend.** New York, New York: Ballantine Books, 1978.

Mandino, Og. **The Greatest Salesman In The World.** Hollywood, Florida: Frederick Fell Publishers, Inc., 1968.

Murphy, Joseph. **How To Attract Money.** Marina Del Ray, California: DeVorss and Company, 1955.

Murphy, Joseph. **Your Infinite Power To Be Rich.** West Nyack, New York: Parker Publishing Company, Inc., 1966.

Patent, Arnold M. **You Can Have It All.** Sylvia, North Carolina: Celebration Publishing, 1991.

Peale, Norman Vincent. **Positive Imaging.** Old Tappan, New Jersey: Fleming H. Revell Company, 1982.

Ponder, Catherine. **The Dynamic Laws Of Prosperity.** Englewood Cliffs, New Jersey: Prentice-Hall, Inc., 1962.

Price, John Randolph. **The Abundance Book.** Boerne, Texas: Quartus Books, 1987.

Proctor, Bob. **You Were Born Rich.** Willowdale, Ontario: McCrary Publishing Inc., 1984.

Rohn, James E. **Seven Strategies For Wealth And Happiness.** Rocklin, California: Prima Publishing And Communications, 1986.

Schuller, Robert H. **Tough Times Don't Last But Tough People Do.** Nashville, Tennessee: Thomas Nelson Publishers, 1983.

Shinn, Florence Scovel. **The Game Of Life.** New York, New York: Simon & Schuster, Inc. 1986.

Shultz, Kennedy. **You Are The Power.** Carson, California: Hay House, Inc., 1993.

Walters, J. Donald. **Money Magnetism.** Nevada City, California: Crystal Clarity Publishers, 1992.

Williamson, Marianne. **A Return To Love.** New York, New York: HarperCollins, Inc. 1992.

Winget, Larry. **The Simple Way To Success.** Tulsa, Oklahoma: Win Publications, 1991.

This is not a complete list. Each of the authors listed have many more excellent books and tapes available that will benefit you greatly. However, this is the best of the best as far as I am concerned. Start here.

Money Is Easy Listening List

Audio Cassette Learning Systems

Jack Boland, **Prosperity Principles That Work,** Master Mind Publishing, 313 756-7050

Eric Butterworth, **Prosperity For You,** The Unity Center, Box 1501, Greenwich, CT 06836

Dr. Deepak Chopra, **Creating Affluence,** Quantum Publications, 508 368-1808

Dr. Wayne Dyer, **Real Magic,** Nightingale Conant, 800 323-5552

Jerry Gillies, **Moneylove,** Nightingale Conant, 800 323-5552

Mark Victor Hansen, **Unlimited Riches,** Mark Victor Hansen & Associates, 800 433-2314

Jim Rohn, **Take Charge Of Your Life,** Nightingale Conant, 800 323-5552

Brian Tracy, **The Universal Laws Of Success And Achievement,** Nightingale Conant, 800 323-5552

Mike Wickett, **Principles for Attracting Riches,** Wickett Corporate Training, 313 644-4944

Marianne Williamson, **Marianne Williamson On Money,** HarperCollins, Publisher - Available at bookstores everywhere

Larry Winget, **The Simple Way To Success,** Win Seminars! 800 749-4597

This is not a complete list. Each of the authors listed have many more audio tape programs available. I heartily recommend anything recorded by anyone listed here.

Larry Winget is a philosopher of success who just happens to be hilarious. He teaches universal principles that will work for anyone, in any business, at any time, and does it by telling funny stories. He believes that most of us have complicated life and business way too much, take it way too seriously and that we need to lighten up, take responsibility, be more flexible, stay positive and keep it in perspective. He believes that success and prosperity come from serving others. He teaches that business improves when the people in the business improve; that everything in life gets better when we get better and nothing gets better until we get better.

To have Larry speak to your organization or to order any of his other personal and professional development products contact :

Win Seminars! Inc.
P. O. Box 700485 • Tulsa, Oklahoma 74170
918.745.6606 • 800.749.4597 • Fax: 918.747.3185

or use the Internet: www.larrywinget.com

Order Form

Books

	Unit Cost	Quantity	Amount
The Simple Way To Success	$12.95	_____	_____
Money Is Easy	$11.95	_____	_____
Stuff That Works Every Single Day	$ 9.95	_____	_____
The Little Red Book Of Stuff That Works	$ 7.95	_____	_____
Just Do This Stuff	$ 7.95	_____	_____
Only The Best On Success	$11.95	_____	_____
Only The Best On Customer Service	$11.95	_____	_____
Only The Best On Leadership	$11.95	_____	_____
Success One Day At A Time	$11.95	_____	_____
That Makes Me Sick!	$7.95	_____	_____
Profound Stuff	$ 9.95	_____	_____
Larry's Library (all ELEVEN above)	$100.00	_____	_____

Other Stuff

	Unit Cost	Quantity	Amount
Shut Up! Stop Whinning And Get A Life *cards* (50)	$ 9.95	_____	_____
Shut Up! Stop Whinning And Get A Life ...*Coffee Mug*	$ 9.95	_____	_____
Stuff That Works ...*Mouse Pad*	$10.95	_____	_____
Shut Up! Stop Whinning And Get A Life ...*Mouse Pad*	$10.95	_____	_____

UNGAWA GEAR

	Unit Cost	Quantity	Amount
Shut Up, Stop Whining And Get A Life *T-shirt (XL only)*	$17.95	_____	_____
UPSIDE DOWN version of above *T-shirt (XL only)*	$17.95	_____	_____
Shut Up, Stop Whining And Get A Life *hat*	$16.95	_____	_____
That Makes Me Sick *T-shirt (XL only)*	$17.95	_____	_____

SHIPPING & HANDLING

If Sub Total is:	USA	Canada
0 - 25.00	$3.00	$ 10.00
25.01 - 100.00	$8.00	$20.00
100.01 - 200.00	$15.00	$30.00
200.01 - 300.00	$25.00	$40.00

Call for rates on purchases over $300.

ALL PRICES U.S. DOLLARS
Canadian Shipping Rates do not include duty, taxes or customs charges that COULD be charged at the border

Sub Total _____
S&H _____
TOTAL _____

Name _____ Date _____

Company _____

STREET Address _____

City/Province _____

Zip/Postal Code _____ Country _____ Day Phone _____

Method of Payment: ☐ AMEX ☐ VISA ☐ Mastercard ☐ Check/Money Order Enclosed

Card No.

Exp. date _____ Signature _____

Win Seminars! Inc. • P.O. Box 700485 • Tulsa, Oklahoma 74170
For Fastest Service Call Toll-Free • **1.800.749.4597** (10:00 am – 3:00 pm, weekdays, CST)
24 Hour Fax Line • **918.747.3185**
Internet • **www.larrywinget.com**

Quantity Discounts are available on all of Larry's Stuff. Call for details.